JOHN KEATS
A Portrait in Words

John Keats
A PORTRAIT IN WORDS

CATHERINE OWENS PEARE

ILLUSTRATED

DODD, MEAD & COMPANY
NEW YORK / 1960

ACKNOWLEDGMENTS

The quotations from John Keats's poetry used in this book are from *The Poetical Works of John Keats*, edited by H. W. Garrod and published by Oxford University Press, London, 1958. The quotations from Keats's letters are to be found in *The Letters of John Keats*, edited by Hyder Edward Rollins and published by Harvard University Press, Cambridge, 1958.

I am indebted to J. H. Preston, Assistant Curator of Keats Memorial House, London, for research assistance; to Mary M. Kenway of The Pierpont Morgan Library and Philip Cohen, M.D., of Brooklyn, New York, for reading the manuscript; and to the following for permission to quote brief passages from the works indicated:

Edmund Blunden: *Leigh Hunt and His Circle*, 1930; *Leigh Hunt's "Examiner" Examined*, 1928.

Oxford University Press, Inc.: *Letters of Fanny Brawne to Fanny Keats 1820-1824*, edited by Fred Edgcumbe, 1937; *Life of John Keats* by Charles Armitage Brown, 1937; *Keats as Doctor and Patient* by Sir William Hale-White, 1938; *The Letters of John Keats,* edited by Maurice Buxton Forman, 1931.

The University of Georgia Press: *Benjamin Robert Haydon, Historical Painter* by Clarke Olney, 1952.

Yale University Press: *Fanny Keats* by Marie Adami, 1938.

Contents

Illustrations

CHAPTER I

Psyche

"JOHN?"

With a sharp and secret twinge of regret he closed the volume of verse and stepped into the sick room in response to the fretful voice. The sight of his mother's wasted face with its unnaturally high color, her dank hair that had once been so lustrous, made him lay down the book altogether. He felt her hand; it was too warm: the temperature of tuberculosis.

"Do you want something, Mother?"

"My son! My dear son!" and she tried to reach out and cling to him.

"Don't exert yourself, Mother. It will bring on a coughing spell."

"Please . . . a drink . . ."

He poured water from the pitcher on the nearby washstand and cradled her head in his arm as he held the cup to her lips. Tenderly he eased her down upon the pillow again.

1

Frances Keats Rawlings gazed up at her fourteen-year-old son with fever-bright eyes.

"You look like your father, John. He was not very tall. Don't worry about not being tall."

"Don't talk any more, Mother. Try to sleep."

He waited until she appeared to doze; then he picked up the copy of Shakespeare's *Sonnets* and left the room, closing the door silently behind him. In the hallway he sat down on the chair, where he had been keeping guard to prevent his younger brothers and sister from disturbing the invalid, and reopened the book.

> When I consider everything that grows
> Holds in perfection but a little moment . . .

Tiny hands laid upon his knee brought the sonnet to a quick end. "John, I want to see Mother."

His sister, Frances Mary, aged six-and-a-half, looked up at him appealingly as she stood there in her long dress, a tiny replica of an adult woman.

"She is sleeping now, Fanny. If you will be patient, I shall take you in to her in a little while."

His brother Tom, aged ten, bounded upon him. "Please let us see her, John. Why can't we see her?"

"You are old enough to understand, Tom. You know she is ill. You may see her when she awakens."

"Are you going back to school?"

"Not until Mother takes a turn for the better," John replied.

"Shall we all stay home?"

"No; you and George will return."

"It's been a dull holiday," observed Tom, lower lip protruding slightly.

"That is no way to talk."

"Grandmother says that Mother is not so ill as you think."

"Don't make any racket," said John Keats as he reopened his book and forgot his two companions. The world around him dissolved, and his imagination was caught up in the rhythm of the iambic pentameter, the compact phrasing, and his lips moved as he felt the pure pleasure of the words upon his tongue.

> Where wasteful Time debateth with Decay,
> To change your day of youth to sullied night . . .

When he had reached the end of the fourteenth line he looked up and found that Fanny and John had left the corridor, but his other brother, twelve-year-old George, stood before him.

"She is still sleeping," John told George.

"Then let her sleep," said George. "Grandmother wants us at table."

John placed the book on the seat of his chair, took a discreet look at the patient, and followed George downstairs.

Mrs. Jennings was already seated at the head of the table, dressed in her severe black widow's dress, her hands folded before her, displaying the only jewelry she allowed herself: her wedding ring and a second gold ring with a black enameled design. In the door to the kitchen stairs stood the maid, a husky, heavy-voiced woman, the only adult in the house of whom the Keats children were cautious. Fanny was already established at her grandmother's right, and the three boys hurried to their chairs, as Mrs. Jennings nodded to the maid to bring in the heavy midday meal: the platter of boiled mutton and greens, the pudding, the coarse loaf, the cheese.

John Keats watched Fanny while she worked clumsily at her plate, and wondered whether he had injured her baby feelings. Of all the family he felt most concerned for her. She had been scarcely a year old when her father died, and so she had been spared that grief; but if now she was to lose her mother . . .

Tom had obviously been thinking along similar lines, for he began to create comic figures in the air with his hands to entertain Fanny. John and George joined in and the meal ended in a round of hilarity.

As soon as they were finished John Keats went below to the kitchen for his mother's tray and carried the slim and scanty diet upstairs: just some porridge and a little tea.

He found her awake, looking remarkably rested, her eyes almost clear, and she smiled pleasantly as he approached her bedside.

"Do you think you can sit up, Mother?"

"Yes, John, if you will help me."

Setting down the tray, he pushed the curtain back against the tall bedpost and slipped both his arms around her, and as he arranged the pillows at her back she kissed him on his cheek.

His mother had always needed love, and her life had been filled with far more yearning than fulfillment. He was her nurse, her father, her mother, her husband, her son, he thought, as he began to lift food to her mouth with the spoon and watched her respond to the tender attention.

"I cannot believe you are so young," she told him.

He was young with young boys, an adult with his mother, as old as Shakespeare when he was reading his poetry . . .

Mrs. Rawlings turned her head to look at the door where Fanny stood.

"May I see Mother now?" asked the child wistfully.

"Let her come to me, John," said Mrs. Rawlings. "I've had enough to eat."

John lifted Fanny up on the bed and watched patiently as she cuddled down into her mother's arms. He let Tom and George come in, too, cautioning them to be quiet and gentle.

After they had had their visit and left, he sat down beside the bed and asked, "Would you like me to read to you?"

"Please, something light . . ."

He read a novel to her until he saw signs of returning fatigue, and then he went downstairs to see his grandmother. The older woman was waiting for him.

"John," she said firmly, "your mother is growing better. I think she is out of danger."

"I shall remain home a few more days."

"No!" Mrs. Jennings announced. "You will return to school with your brothers. I can take care of your mother."

"I shall remain!" he retorted with sudden anger. He had been head of the family too long to be ordered about like a boy. His face became flushed, his eyes blazed, his pulse raced.

His grandmother beat a quick retreat and spoke to him in a gentle, persuasive tone. "John, I only want you to return because I can see that your mother is out of danger. Enfield isn't far from here. We can easily fetch you back if she grows worse. She has been ill for several years, John. First it was rheumatism, now her lungs. She will be ill for many more years. Now, tell me. Did she eat any supper?"

"Yes, she did eat something, Grandmother."

"There! You see?"

In his own heart he believed he saw improvement in his mother's condition, and perhaps it was enough to justify his return to Enfield.

Their Christmas holiday concluded, the three Keats brothers set out together on a dark, chill January morning. They left the Jennings house, standing primly on the south side of Church Street in Edmonton, and walked down the curving street to the village green. All three thought longingly of the pond at its farthest end, but there was no time now. They sought the inn where the stage coaches and stage wagons stopped and eased their bundles to the ground to await their vehicle, the slower but cheaper wagon.

At last the clumsy Enfield stage wagon appeared, drawn by its pairs of tired, naglike horses, the driver plodding along at the head of the lead pair. It stopped only long enough to discharge some passengers and take the Keats boys aboard.

They jogged over the frost-hardened road for nearly an hour, watching the dawn break and the hedged and pastoral countryside grow gradually visible. Enfield, about two miles north of Edmonton, was a cluster of houses along the road with a church in their midst. The boys jumped down in front of the Greyhound Inn, accomplishing the school building at a fast trot.

As John Keats rushed through the door in the center of the two-story-and-an-attic red brick building and into the big wooden corridor, he became a boy again, happily greeting other boys who were appearing from everywhere. Adult burdens fell away; he reveled in his popularity. Other students seemed to feel an instinctive respect for him, and he knew it. He'd fought many of them, often bested lads bigger than himself, and there was no need here to worry about not being tall enough—not any more.

He hurried toward Charles Cowden Clarke, son of John Clarke the headmaster. Charles Clarke, one of the instructors, was only twenty-two years old, endowed with the gift of youth-understanding-youth and a scholar's sympathy for searching young minds. Clarke was smiling and nodding greetings to all the boys, but his face lighted up as soon as he saw John Keats.

"My dear fellow! I hope you left all well at home."

"Pretty well, I think, Mr. Clarke. Mother seemed to be recovering."

"You look a little at a loss for sleep."

"I sat up with her one or two nights."

The boys trooped upstairs with their bundles to the dormitory rooms—six, seven, and eight beds to a room—and then downstairs again and across a yard to a smaller building whose interior served as a classroom, forty feet long. The two buildings had once been the private home and coachhouse of a wealthy merchant.

John Keats lost track of his brothers as he sought his class group at a long table flanked by backless benches. The room was filled with the excitement and commotion of returning. It was hard for the boys to adjust so suddenly to the quiet concentration of learning, but the instructors and their assisting ushers were patiently giving the energy time to wear down.

"What did you read over the holiday?" asked young Clarke when he stopped near John Keats's table.

"Mostly Shakespeare's *Sonnets* this time. But not many of them, I am afraid."

"You will have more opportunity here."

The yell of a young student caused John Keats to look up suddenly, his eyes fiery.

"Not one of your brothers, Keats," said Clarke with a marked note of amusement. "One of the lower-form boys having his ears boxed by an upperclassman."

Had it been Tom or George, John Keats would have been out of his seat, fists doubled up, and after the offender.

Clarke drifted away to hear the spelling lesson of a lower group, and Keats turned his attention to the volume of the *Aeneid* before him and the handwritten pages of translation he had already accomplished. He usually felt no ardor for knowledge that had to be gleaned from another language, but this book—this author—offered rhythm, tempo, action. At fourteen Keats's knowledge of Latin had become quite good, so the translation task was only moderately laborious, and most certainly rich in inspiration. A writer who could produce page after page of such splendid and heroic verse, filled with vivid and courageous characters, must be a very special kind of person, endowed above all other men.

The last vestiges of the gloomy moods of home were submerged in the pleasures of mind and young company as John moved from class to class, and the pure joy of thinking and imagining drove his spirits higher and higher. When at last the long school schedule disgorged its charges upon the out-of-doors, he bolted wildly with the wild herd across the playground, along the edge of the school's vegetable garden behind it, to the pond, the meadows, and beyond them all to the New River that curved in a loop around Enfield before it pursued its course to London.

English schoolboys turned loose in January 1810 immediately sailed under Nelson or commanded a battalion for Wellington. Napoleon was at the zenith of his power, and England stood alone against him. The Battle of Trafalgar was four years old, and even without his navy the ruthless conqueror had gone on to bring Europe to her knees.

It was also the time of the Whigs and Tories, and older boys who had lost their taste for sham battles could argue and wrangle over privilege and reform, and if they finished locked in a bruising tussle and rolling over the ground, there would be time enough for democratic self-restraints. The volatile John Keats returned at the end of recreation time, his stockings and knee breeches and jacket as dirty and disheveled as his companions', to wash vaguely at the pump in the yard, without benefit of soap or towel.

But by suppertime he was lost in the printed page again, for the understanding and tolerant Clarkes allowed him to read at table, let him read anything he wished, suggested titles, loaned him the volumes: Joseph Spence's *Polymetis*, a comparative study of the Roman poets and their predecessors; a translation of the Latin poet, Ovid; John Lemprière's

Classical Dictionary, filled with answers to Keats's questions on mythology and classical history; histories ancient and modern.

The weeks at school were a balm, and the loss of sleep was made up, the tensions eased. January gave way to February with its still frosty though more temperate weather and its days nearly two hours longer. The beginning of March brought cold rains and winds. Soon he would be able to go out into the corner of the garden where plots were reserved for the students and plant anything he wished. The earliest days of spring would bring flowers out on the perennial shrubs and blossoms on the fruit trees, and all the meadows and nearby woods would turn a deep, rich green; the red brown dust of the roadway would glow like gold in the afternoon sun.

Between the March showers, often ignoring the mist that gathered in iridescent droplets on his jacket, John Keats roamed the paths and the bank of the river, delighting in every kind of creation and growth he could find. He was lying on his stomach on the river bank one day when an underclassman came running toward him all out of breath to say that John Keats was wanted in the headmaster's office. Rinsing his hands, John got to his feet and trudged back to the schoolhouse, begrudging every minute of the day that he was losing.

"Come in, Keats," said Mr. John Clarke, and his voice was filled with gentle sympathy.

A loving hand was laid upon John's shoulder—a few preparatory words—and he had the tragic news. His mother had died.

She'd been *worse*, not better, as he had believed when he returned to school! She'd been dying then in all probability. She'd been . . .

Sudden, shocking grief swirled around him and swept him

into confusion. Choking, sobbing, unseeing, he was guided toward a chair, but he broke away.

"Come, Keats! Death is something that everyone must learn to face."

"They told me . . . they told me she was getting well . . . I thought she . . ."

And he crumbled down, down . . . When hands reached out to lift him up, he struggled and scrambled away, found the headmaster's desk, crawled under it out of reach, and lay there sobbing and shaking.

Not until much later could he be led back to his bed and persuaded to rest. When he awoke from dozing he saw his brothers sitting on either side of him; their eyes were red, their faces forlorn. He tried to rise, but his head was too heavy and aching, and he fell back upon the pillow.

"We must go home, John," said George.

"Do you think you can stand the ride?" asked Tom. "Mr. Abbey has come for us in his yellow landau."

Richard Abbey, a friend of their grandmother's, appeared in the household from time to time, giving pompous advice. He was stout and endowed with the kind of vulgarness that is automatically offensive to children. George didn't mind him too much, but John Keats closed his eyes at the mention of the man's name.

As soon as John was able he and his brothers climbed into the vehicle beside its corpulent owner and jogged homeward. They found the house on Church Street bustling with neighbors, and Grandmother Jennings sat in a large chair with Fanny dozing in her lap. The child's face was puffed and stained as though she had cried herself to sleep.

"I want to see Mother," John announced as he walked in.

"Not just now, John," his grandmother told him.

"She is being cared for," said Mr. Abbey. "You can see her later, tomorrow perhaps."

Neither anger nor anguish did him any good. All he had was the sudden sense that he had lost control of things, lost control chiefly to Abbey, who walked about the house as though he were its master.

On March 20, 1810, a subdued and solemn party of mourners accompanied Frances Jennings Keats Rawlings to London and buried her in the Keats family plot beside her first husband, Thomas Keats, at the little Wren-designed church of St. Stephen on the west side of Coleman Street.

The dimly lighted interior, the finely carved oak pulpit, the darkened oak of the panels and pews, all suited John Keats's mood, even though the service could not hold his attention. He had long ago fallen into the habit of letting his fancy wander where it would when he was in church, whether in the old Edmonton church where his grandmother took the brood on Sunday morning, or here, or anywhere for that matter.

John Keats had already lost any real taste for the formalities of church.

CHAPTER II

Lag, Lag, Laglast!

BUT HIS ONCE YOUNG and vivacious mother, the now deceased Frances Jennings, had had sufficient taste for church when, nearly sixteen years before, on an October day in 1794, she had gone to the larger and more fashionable St. George's in Hanover Square to be married to Thomas Keats. Frances had been the daughter of John Jennings, owner of the prosperous Swan and Hoop livery stables at 28 Finsbury Pavement, London, and the groom was his head foreman and chief hostler. It was just as well, for John Jennings's only surviving son had no taste for the business and had sought a career in the Marines. Frances had secured to the business a most capable manager, a man who *knew* horses in a day when horses were an indispensable part of everyone's life.

Frances and Thomas Keats were well matched, both filled with animal spirits and the sheer physical pleasure of being alive, both attractive, both middle class with a tinge of *nouveau riche* in their tastes and ambitions. What Thomas

Keats lacked in height he made up for in physical strength, and what Frances Jennings Keats lacked in subtle refinement she compensated for with her blooming vitality.

The couple lived, during the first two or three years of their married life, with Frances Keats's parents in their rooms over the livery stable. The quarters were ample enough and in keeping with their prosperity, but filled with the odors and hurly-burly of the stables beneath. Since every sound represented a profit, who could complain or mind?

And none did until the birth of their first child, John, on October 31, 1795. Then the young parents began to feel more conscious of gentility and the acute lack of it in Finsbury Pavement. They even began to chat glibly of Harrow for the boy.

John Keats was scarcely a year old when his entire family situation underwent a revision that moved them socially upward. His grandparents, John and Alice Jennings, turned over the business to their son-in-law and retired to a house in the village of Ponders End, very close to Enfield, and about nine miles north of the Swan and Hoop. His parents, Thomas and Frances Jennings Keats, took a house in Craven Street, a half mile north of the stables.

Craven Street, short and narrow, turned out of City Road, providing an east-west connection between City Road and the Bishopgate–Shoreditch route out of London to Ponders End and Enfield. The Keats house was one in a row of attached houses, brick, three stories high, all monotonously similar to one another. But such things are a question of degree, and Thomas and Frances Keats bought furniture and set up housekeeping with gusto, and with the same kind of gusto their adored and pampered first-born began to grow up, self-willed and tempestuous, almost a stranger to discipline.

In February of 1797, when John Keats was a year and four

months old, Thomas and Frances Keats had their second child, a boy named George; and in November 1799, when John was four, their third child, another boy, named Thomas.

Those early years were happy, prosperous, unspoiled, filled with promise; Thomas Keats's management of the Swan and Hoop was highly competent; life in the Craven Street house was amiable and plenteous. On a Sunday or holiday the Keatses could climb into their own carriage, pulled by a spanking fine pair of horses, the best the livery stable could obtain, and drive to Ponders End for a visit, out over the Great Northern Road through the gently rolling countryside, past open fields, patches of wood, through the villages of Tottenham and Edmonton, now and then catching a glimpse of the Lea River on their right.

For John Keats a visit to his grandparents meant running free in gloriously natural surroundings. A rushing charge through tall grass could scare birds up into sudden flight. A hunt on all fours through shrubs revealed an ever-growing list of insect forms and small animals, and an excursion along the ditch that followed a hedgerow was bound to disclose a rabbit's burrow.

"John! John!" . . . and the boy exploring the hedgerow lifted his head and listened without responding to his grandfather's voice. Grandfather Jennings loved to eat; he was in a hurry for dinner. "John! John!" No matter when he returned to the house, Mother or Grandmother would surely feed him. He felt no need to worry.

"Oh, he will come for *me*," he heard another voice say. "John! John!"

That was Mother. Yes, he would come to Mother. He leaped up and bolted toward the sound, rushing pell-mell into her open arms and winding his own arms tightly around her neck as she swung him from the ground and carried him gayly into the house.

The visits at Ponders End were exciting and satisfying, in a world that held more for John Keats than the city ever could. The multifooted creature that squirmed in his palm and crawled up his arm, the bird calls he was learning to identify, the wild flowers that refused to delay their life-spans for him—these were the ultimate of living—these were life.

Yet, back on the paved fringe of London there was excitement of its own kind. He could easily find his way to the Swan and Hoop to be told by the handlers and sweepers to stand back out of harm's way. Son of the manager, John Keats was as protected there as with his mother. If he showed a curiosity about wandering deeper into the narrow, crowded, busy, dirty, raucous streets of eighteenth-century London, someone at the Swan and Hoop was bound to go after him and take him home.

Home was considerably less attractive at times, particularly when he was told to be quiet, that mother wasn't feeling well. It happened every once in a while—Mother's retirement to her bedroom during the day—and the oldest boy quickly fell into the role of defending her against disturbers, sometimes with a toy sword in hand.

In April 1801 a fourth boy, Edward, was born, but Edward never came within the sphere of John's experience. A weak, frail infant, he survived only a few months. Did he die? John wanted to know. Yes, that was it. What was death? Not anything very real, certainly, and not anything John was obliged to think about.

The next and last baby was not born until June 1803, when John was almost eight: Frances Mary Keats, who quickly became "Fanny," the doll-like baby sister. John felt that he shared with his father some of the responsibility for her, but his father took another view of it and told him that he would not be at home enough to look after her, that he was to begin school. But he knew his letters! Mother was teaching

him! That was not sufficient, Thomas Keats explained carefully. He wanted John to learn a great deal more than either
his mother or his father could teach him; he wanted John
to amount to something, to be a fine gentleman. John Keats
was to be entered with his brother George at a private school
in Enfield, very close to Ponders End and their grandparents.

The thought of separation from the house that had always
been the center of his universe was shocking, but there was
no altering the decision. Sober-faced and silent from fear,
John and George perched on the carriage seat beside their
father as Thomas Keats drove them to their doom.

The yard before the school was crowded with horses and
carriages and the hallways swarmed with boys as John and
George entered, each clinging to one of Thomas's hands. Arrangements had already been made. Today was merely a
matter of being turned over to a strange, rather strait-laced
man called the Headmaster, one Mr. John Clarke, who in
turn put them in charge of his own son, Charles Cowden
Clarke.

When John Keats placed his hand in that of young Clarke,
only eight years older than himself, his fears began to dissolve.

"It's really not such a bad place here," said Clarke cheerfully. "My father doesn't believe in teaching with the rod,
and if you do very well he will give you a fine prize."

"What kind of prize, Mr. Clarke?" asked John Keats.

"Oh, various things. Sometimes a book, sometimes an en-
graved medal. But it's always something really worth having.
Come. Let me show you both where you will sleep."

The prizes about which Clarke had told him did not come
John's way during his first years, because there were too many
other things at Enfield just as interesting as books and totally
removed from the classroom. There was a new kind of social
life in which his nimble energy and spontaneous generosity,
together with his oldest-boy-in-the-family boldness, won him

a quick place. His quick rages when he was thwarted became a legend, and Charles Cowden Clarke once laughed and said that his temper was "picturesque." Another instructor labeled him the "little terrier" because of his courage and readiness to fight anyone regardless of size. Out-of-doors there was further competition for his lessons, as he renewed and increased his acquaintance with the flora and fauna that he had begun to discover at Ponders End. He was still young enough that first year at Enfield to make toy boats and sail them on the New River on "visionary seas," or sit and watch the diving swans, never to lose the memory of the image; or feel all violence vanish from his soul as he came upon a nest of half-fledged thrushes.

The remarkably progressive teaching of the Clarkes gradually identified the things John Keats loved with the things he read. Easy lessons in astronomy interpreted the night sky, the principal constellations and their imaginative pagan names, the precision with which they rose and set. A touch of botany revealed the workmanship in the flowers. But there was still no passion in the way he completed his lessons, and he did not go beyond his assignments in Latin, numbers, geography, geometry. One of his best exposures at Enfield was to contemporary French, since the French Revolution had sent many high-caste Frenchmen scurrying to other lands for safety, and the Clarke school had its native French instructor. John Keats acquired a real facility in the language, particularly in reading it.

But for him and all the boys in the lower form, who had not yet felt even a first glimmer of their adolescence, there was no substitute for the out-of-doors. They spent their accumulated energies racing over the meadows when the school day was done, or gathered at sunset to watch the familiar swarm of rooks that came sweeping home over their heads, black plumage glistening purple in the half-light, caw-

ing and crying toward their long-established rookery near
the school. "Lag, lag, laglast!" shouted the boys, as the big
birds swept by on slow-beating wings, seeking their nests
in the early spring, or roosting in nearby trees when the
mating season was done.

The rooks had not yet forsaken their nests in the middle
of April 1804, when John and George Keats were abruptly
summoned home from school. They were snatched from
the midst of their classes, driven at high speed, and led into a
house filled with gloom. Frances Keats, her face tear-stained
and her eyes red, rushed and hugged them to her, bursting
into fresh weeping.

"Your father—your father rode to Southgate—merely for
dinner—dinner with a client . . ."

The room seemed to be milling with people, and John
Keats, looking up into the sad faces around him, became
acutely aware of one he did not like: that of the paunchy
Richard Abbey. John withdrew from Abbey's outstretched
hand with the uninhibited candor of childhood.

Thomas Keats had set off for Southgate, Abbey told John,
riding one of his own horses, a splendid mount. On the return trip—he was only two miles or so from home—the horse
skidded on the cobblestone pavement and pitched his rider
headlong into an iron fencing. The night watchman making
his rounds found Thomas Keats lying there conscious, but
unable to speak, and took the injured man to a nearby house
until he could be identified. He died that same morning.

Death became a sudden, shocking reality, a force that could
move swiftly as lightning and change the whole pattern of
living, remove this essential person or that, foist new responsi-
bilities upon those unequal to the task. John's mother was
now mistress of the Swan and Hoop as well as of her home
and four small children, and she would not have had the

stability for it in any century, let alone the beginning of the nineteenth.

The house in Craven Street suffered an acute lack of organization during the days following the funeral; there were sudden emotional outbursts from the lonely, love-starved, twenty-nine-year-old Mrs. Keats, outbursts that upset everyone down to the youngest. It all had a profoundly maturing effect upon John, who felt himself a diminutive head of the house, and he was startled to be told he must return to school.

"Who will take care of *you?*" John wanted to know.

"Oh," hinted his mother, turning on her most winsome smile, "you must remember that Mother has many friends."

Once back at school, a chief source of comfort for the two Keats boys was their grandparents at Ponders End, and they visited them frequently. On occasion, Mr. and Mrs. Jennings drove to the school, but not very often, since the effort was so costly to the aging Mr. Jennings. Looking at his failing grandfather, John Keats, aware of a new factor in life, wondered when death would reach him. What would become of *that* household when death took away its ruling head?

On one of his walks to Ponders End, John Keats bounded into the house to find his whole family gathered—his mother, five-year-old Tom, one-year-old Fanny—all looking happy, eager and excited. They had good news for him, they said. Here was someone he was to meet and like, someone—this stranger—Mr. William Rawlings—mother's new husband—John's stepfather.

A mere ten and a half weeks after her first husband's death, the emotionally dependent Frances Jennings Keats had married again. Mr. Rawlings was a bank clerk, scarcely the executive type, yet he was going to resign his position and take over the running of the Swan and Hoop. The new Mrs. Rawlings explained to her four children that she wanted them to remain with their grandparents for a little while.

John Keats's "picturesque" temper flared up hot and he turned upon the stranger, the interloper. "You're taking her away, and we will never see her again!"

No, no, no, it was not to be like that. The arrangement was merely for a while, and then they would all be together. Mother and Mr. Rawlings would be just a few miles away in London, near the Swan and Hoop. Persistently they talked to him until his rage cooled and he began to accept the new separation.

"Tom will join you at school next term," Mrs. Rawlings promised her son, "and then there will be three of you at Enfield. Grandmother will take care of Fanny."

John looked at Tom in a loving, paternalistic way. Tom was the sickly type; John would have to be on the alert to stand between him and the older, stronger boys.

Tom did come, just as his mother had promised, and so there were three Keats brothers to come trudging to Ponders End for their school holidays, to beg for news of their mother, or to hope that Mother would be there, and to overwhelm the baby Fanny with attention and help her improve her ability to walk and talk.

But once again the pattern of living did not endure for long, and early in March the Jennings household was disrupted by the death of John Jennings. It was not so shocking as the death of his son-in-law had been, because he was old and had gradually foretold it in his shrinking physique and failing interest, but it did transplant the four Keats children to yet a third home. Alice Jennings with her bevy of grandchildren moved to a house on Church Street in Edmonton.

John rather felt that he knew Edmonton, for on every drive from London either to Enfield or Ponders End their carriage or stage had passed through the village. It was a two-mile walk from Enfield, but through the same kind of interesting terrain. Pymme's Brook crossed under the road at Edmonton and found its way through boggy meadows to the Lea River, and both the brook and the river offered an abundance of minnows, frogs, aquatic beetles, miller's-thumb, and dace, while the meadows sheltered mice, goldfinches, and warblers. The indulgent grandmother allowed John to keep his water-dwelling pets in a washing tub in the yard.

The adjustment from house to house and village to village wasn't really hard, since school life remained constant, and even at ten John Keats did not wonder how such things were financed. There had always been enough money coming from somewhere as far as he was aware. Actually John Jennings had left his wife with a comfortable living, a capital fund yielding her about two hundred pounds a year, and he had established another fund providing his daughter with about fifty pounds a year that was to go to her children after her death. In addition he left a thousand pounds directly to his grandchildren to be divided and distributed as each came of age. But the stables had been a dowry to his daughter, John Keats's mother, and under the property laws of the times Rawlings had acquired possession of them by marrying her.

The Swan and Hoop was earning less and less under its bank-clerk manager-owner, but the Keats brothers were too young to be aware of that. They lived their rough-and-tumble lives at the Clarke school in Enfield, consenting to learn only what was required of them. Tom made a quick adjustment, and John, who had a capacity for enjoying friendships on almost any age level, accepted the youngest boys attracted to Tom, at the same time that his friendship with Charles Cowden Clarke was deepening. Tom was special because—four years younger—he needed understanding and encouragement; Charles Cowden Clarke was special because—eight years older—he gave these things.

Clarke had the vision and insight to see the scholar in John Keats long before Keats was aware of it himself. Clarke had become his intimate counselor, wisely guiding his temperament into creative expression, instead of attempting to frustrate it. He brought the most imaginative literary works to Keats's attention, read with him to encourage the habit, showed deep interest in his family life, became a source of comfort in time of tragedy.

It was to Clarke that Keats turned, upon Clarke whom he flung himself, when returning to Enfield after a school holiday. In Edmonton he had found his mother ill, brokenhearted, destitute of everything except the fifty pounds a year her father had recently left her.

"She had to leave that Rawlings fellow!" Keats told Clarke. "He must have driven her out of the house with his evil ways. I'm sure he abused her! I think he just married her to get her property."

"That happens too often to well-to-do widows," Clarke agreed. "Can your grandmother take care of her?"

"Oh, yes!" Keats burst out. "She will remain with us. She is never going back to *him*. I won't let her."

CHAPTER III

A Young Horse in a Spring Meadow

HIS MOTHER'S SPIRIT was broken by her succession of experiences, and health slowly succumbed to the spirit. She had begun to suffer from rheumatism, and as the physical pain grew more intense and crippling she resigned herself to it and soon was a bedridden invalid, needing care, attention, pampering. Upon John, her oldest son, the child who had had the best of her love in her happiest years, she called again and again for bedside service whenever he was home on a holiday.

"You are stronger than Grandmother," she would say. "Spare her steps, whenever you can."

Inevitably John slipped gradually into the role of head of the family; his mother drew comfort and security from laying a hand on his arm; his younger brothers and sister accepted his judgment and direction. He gave generously of his devotion, living in a state of anxiety most of the time that he was in the house, and eagerly hurried back to the more wholesome boys' world of the Enfield school.

23

Charles Cowden Clarke and his other instructors continued to court his interest with the masters, sometimes reminding him of prizes available, but even at twelve they could not lure him beyond the required curriculum. The spark lay dormant within him, unkindled, awaiting the full flush of adolescent fervor to ignite it and the romantic revival in English letters to fan it into full flame.

Clarke was no literary prophet; he had no notion whatever of nurturing a new name for English letters. Clarke was simply an enlightened, compassionate teacher who knew and wanted to share with any student showing a capacity for it the deep happiness to be found in books; and when John Keats in his fourteenth year finally qualified for a prize, the Clarkes presented him with a book suitable to his station in life: Kaufmann's *Dictionary of Merchandise.*

Since Keats was no literary prophet either, he was happily stimulated by the prize, and it was nicely timed, for he was beginning to be a voluntary reader. Other prizes could be won for taking on extra assignments, and since Keats's knowledge of Latin was at last adequate enough Clarke wisely guided him to the *Aeneid* of Virgil, and Keats began a translation. Whenever Clarke's duties permitted, they sat and read Shakespeare together.

News of each bit of progress at school John Keats reported happily to his family, and the smile he could win from his mother was as gratifying as the awards themselves. If only his mother could recover, if only she could be encouraged to rise from her bed, to dress becomingly once more! But each time he came home she seemed a little weaker, thinner, more wasted, less interested in what went on about her, and she coughed rather often.

"I think we must have another doctor," he said to his grandmother.

The doctor was adequate, Alice Jennings reassured him;

and then she gave him the news that his mother's affliction was not merely rheumatism. Frances Jennings Keats Rawlings had the consumption.

"But Mother is young! Is she going to die? Are we going to lose her altogether?"

Mrs. Jennings only patted his hand in a dear-God-I-don't-know sort of way, and they sat and talked of other things—his brothers, the baby Fanny, the prize he'd won—then back to his mother waiting for him to come up to her. Talking was an escape valve . . .

"Go up to her, John, and try not to show your feelings."

Never had he felt his lack of years and his lack of stature so acutely. He wanted to be a man—quickly!—to be done with growing up so that he could take on this new responsibility. As he opened the door to her room, Frances Keats Rawlings moved back the curtain of her bed with a limp hand. Her eyes were red; she'd been crying. So she knew! If she knew and he knew and she had already been weeping, what feelings were there not to show? What was there to conceal? Impulsively he rushed into the room and fell on the edge of the bed, wrapped his arms around her and buried his face in the side of her neck, as they both cried and cried afresh, letting their emotions run out upon the air until their relief was complete.

He would look after her; he would give her her medicines; he would bring her meal trays. He hurried back downstairs, and the maid-of-all-work who was such a martinet could no longer terrify him. Boldly he stood up to her and even invaded the sacred precincts of her kitchen to supervise the preparation of Mrs. Rawlings's food.

When he returned to Enfield it was to seek both solace and exhilaration in study and reading, until books became the end and all of living. When he had exhausted the school library, Clarke began lending him volumes from the family's private collection: works from every literate century, many of them popular contemporaries. After Shakespeare, Keats sensed a lack of substance in Sir Walter Scott and felt pleased that he had the power of discernment. He came upon other romantic writers who did possess great substance—Rousseau, the early William Wordsworth—and felt their spiritual kinship to the French Revolution and their literary heritage from the Elizabethan era. These great men in sharing their wisdom with him made him feel wise—and mature.

In October 1809, John Keats was fourteen; in March 1810, his mother died, and by the time the four Keats children were being driven back to Edmonton from the burial at St. Stephen's, John Keats with his tremendous resilience was beginning to recover from the shock, and think of his responsibility to the other three.

He and his brothers soon learned that Mrs. Jennings, aged seventy-four and sensible of how little life span remained to her, had made permanent provision for all four Keats children by placing them under the guardianship of two trustees: the inevitable Richard Abbey whom she had known for many years, and one John Rowland Sandell. The trust included the thousand pounds that her husband had left to the four children, and to it she added eight thousand pounds of her own.

The immediate effect on John, his brothers and sister was that Abbey was a more frequent visitor than ever before, driving over from his home in nearby Walthamstow, sometimes bringing his wife and adopted daughter with him. Sandell went off to Europe, and they heard practically nothing from him; but Abbey—and even his wife—exercised jurisdiction over the Keats brood with a real relish.

"These children seem rather indolent," was Mrs. Abbey's observation. "They've had far too little discipline."

The observation possessed considerable truth, but it also portended ill.

Abbey allowed the Keats brothers to continue at Enfield, but John and George both knew it would not be for much longer. Abbey was a merchant, not a scholar, and he thought in terms of a man's ability to turn a profit. When John brought home a silver medal that he had won for the prodigious amount of reading he had done, Abbey weighed it in his hand for its value as a coin, snorting a bit at the point of view that valued the engraving above the metal. When John's next prize proved to be John Bonnycastle's *Introduction to Astronomy*, the weight of Abbey's trusteeship grew heavier. By the end of the summer term of 1811 both John and George could expect to leave the enchanted climes of Enfield and begin apprenticeships.

But he had not yet finished his translation of the *Aeneid!* John thought. How could he explain that to a tea merchant? Wisely he decided not to, and he was surprised to learn that Abbey had enough respect for his scholarly leanings to apprentice him to a profession—even a profession for which he had shown some aptitude. He was to study under Dr. Thomas Hammond, the surgeon and apothecary who lived on the same street in Edmonton as Mrs. Jennings.

George and Tom were not going to have such a pleasant time of it. They were to be made into sharp merchants in Abbey's own establishment at 4 Pancras Lane, London; George now and Tom in the near future.

In spite of his frank and intense dislike of Abbey, a cunning side in John Keats's nature responded favorably to his own arrangement. The fat codger had been almost amiable about it, for if Keats could remain in Edmonton he really did not have to give up Enfield and Charles Cowden Clarke. He did rather feel some vocation for tending the sick, although he had never been called upon to tend anyone whom he did not love.

Medicine was certainly a few notches above the tea business. George and Tom wouldn't be so far away, and he would be able to go up to London to see them on occasion. One day they'd all be of age, and then Abbey could go hang!

John Keats moved into the second-floor room of a little box of a cottage alongside of Dr. Hammond's ample, ivy-covered home. In the room beneath his own, called "the surgery," Keats learned to do professional chores. He compounded medicines, fashioned pills, prepared dressings and instruments, studied anatomy and dissected vertebrates. He took his meals with the doctor's family.

The newness of the situation and change of study methods engrossed him for a while and kindled his imagination. He really did have to do something for a living. Why not this? Some days he went about with the doctor on his calls, held the horse when the situation inside was too intimate for a sixteen-year-old lad, went into the sick room whenever the doctor permitted. Standing beside Hammond at the bedside of a patient while the doctor made reassuring remarks was deeply nostalgic for Keats, especially if the patient was a woman whose hair had lost its luster in illness, and whose eyes lighted up at every hopeful word.

"Hope is a strong medicine," the doctor counseled Keats.

Hope was in fact one of the few constructive medical techniques of the eighteenth century. Others were the application of live leeches, crude purges of senna and castor oil, cupfuls of loathsome brews, doses of port wine, poultices laid upon every kind of swelling and lump; and blood-letting was the favorite end-all and cure-all. Keats would eventually have to learn how to select a good vein in the arm or the foot, open it, and draw off blood into a cup. As much as a pint could be taken at one time and the procedure was repeated in one or two hours.

Keats's tasks as an apprentice were not at all taxing. Dr.

Hammond allowed him a great deal of free time to sit in his room and read or continue his translation of the *Aeneid*. His five years of apprenticeship were going to be pleasant years, he soon realized, as his routine became established. He could walk up Church Street to his grandmother's house almost any afternoon and inquire for a letter from George or Tom, and he could romp with Fanny, wondering a little sheepishly whether he really was eight years older than she or merely another eight-year-old.

But he knew his true maturity on those days when he strode happily along the two miles of country road back to Enfield to seek out Clarke's home, pausing a short distance away to listen to tinkling sounds of the pianoforte that Clarke enjoyed playing.

"My dear John, come in!"

Keats wanted to talk about Ovid this time, because Charles Cowden Clarke had given him at the time of his departure from Enfield a copy of the Latin poet's *Metamorphoses* translated into English. Keats had been surprised by the lightheartedness of the ancient writer. He felt deeply curious about his verse structures.

"Those are elegiacs," Clarke explained, "or rather the form used by the ancient Greeks and Romans for their elegies."

They talked and talked about the ancient fables retold in the *Metamorphoses*—Apollo, Daphne, Isis, Narcissus, Echo, Pygmalion—and of Ovid himself, high-caste Roman citizen of the days of the Emperor Augustus.

When Keats departed he took home with him a fresh supply of volumes from the Clarke family library, having returned those he had recently finished.

During the short winter evenings Keats and Clarke sat indoors, burning costly candles to supplement the light from the fireplace so that they could read together. It was Clarke who usually did the reading aloud. In the longer spring and

early summer evenings they strolled to the meadow behind
the school to sit in the shelter of an arbor fashioned of sapling
branches, and now and again the song of a nightingale
punctuated the lines of some poet.

They declaimed *Cymbeline* upon the summer air during
Keats's first year of apprenticeship to Hammond—a romantic story for young and sentimental romanticists.

When Mary Tighe's posthumous volume of saccharine verse
came out and enjoyed a temporary glory, John Keats reveled
in it. His eyes lighted quickly upon the sonnet, "To My
Mother," and the tender identification was made. He read
through canto after canto of *Psyche*, carefully studying Mrs.
Tighe's Italian-style stanzas. Shakespearean and Miltonian ex-
cellence were beyond his reach, but suddenly in his hand he
had a successful though mediocre writer, and almost unconsciously he began to realize that writing was possible to
anyone, that the fashioning of verse was something that anyone dared try.

But it was Edmund Spenser, through Clarke the wise
teacher, who gave Keats his initial conscious direction. One
evening, when his friend opened a book from which he was
going to read, Keats asked,

"What is it to be this time, Charles?"

"A nuptial song, Spenser's *Epithalamion*."

"Was he in love when he wrote it?"

"Deeply. He designed it as a monument to his second wife,
just after their marriage."

John Keats sat back with his eyes half shut while Clarke
began:

> Ye learnèd sisters, which have oftentimes
> Beene to me ayding, others to adorne,
> Whom ye thought worthy of your gracefull rymes,
> That even the greatest did not greatly scorne

To heare theyr names sung in your simple layes,
But joyèd in theyr praise . . .

When he had concluded the first group of eighteen lines, Clarke looked up and found Keats's face alive with happiness, his eyes wide open and sparkling.

"Spenser!" said Keats. "Of course! Why haven't I read him before this?"

"For the same reason that you have not yet read many other poets: you cannot read with one book in each hand."

"Go on with Spenser's marriage day."

Clarke obeyed happily, and soon Keats interrupted him impulsively.

"That meter . . ."

"The iambic pentameter?"

"Yes, but pretend it's dactyl for a moment. Emphasize the first word in each line: '*Do* you awake' and '*Go* to the bower' and '*Wake* now my love.' Do you see?"

Clarke nodded.

"Does he usually use iambic pentameter?" Keats asked.

"Yes, usually."

"And so did Shakespeare," Keats mused.

After the poem was concluded, they talked late into the evening about it, its imagery, its use of folklore, its lyric cadences. When Keats set out on his two-mile walk back to Edmonton he had tucked under his arm a copy of Spenser's *The Faerie Queene*.

Next morning, with one backward glance at the new volume, Keats went to the doctor's breakfast table, then with the doctor in his carriage to visit patients, and thus from one task to another through a typical day. Sometimes instructor and apprentice got on well together, and just as often they did not. Keats had a strong ego, a dignity sensitive to patronage. The doctor, thinking he dealt with a boy, occasionally found himself plunged into a sudden hot conflict. Keats could learn from a friend, share literary delights, wait eagerly upon Clarke's judgment as he was led from poet to poet; but he could not play with any ease the naïve role of teen-age boy accepting knowledge doled out by the adult world. Life had rushed him too rapidly beyond that phase.

Eagerly he hurried away from the doctor's explanations and directions, from the complaining voices of his patients, from the laboratory tasks, vaulted up the stairs to his room in the cottage, and seized the volume of Spenser. He became lost in the rich language in an instant, and before he had read half a dozen pages he was caught up in the narrative, the characterizations, the imagery, the allegory, the mysticism. Now and again Keats repeated a line aloud to heighten its melody.

He came upon the creature turned into a tree by a curse, a tree still human enough to bleed when its bows were rent. In a free imagination anything was possible! By the third canto Keats was reading of the maiden so pure she halted the "ramping lyon" who forgot his savage hunger at the sight of her purity and innocence:

> In stead thereof he kist her wearie feet,
> And lickt her lilly hands with fawning tong . . .

Poet there was in Keats, but the poet was housed in a rough country boy; he enjoyed the lurid Elizabethan coarseness too:

> Therewith she spewd out of her filthie maw
> A floud of poyson horrible and blacke . . .

All during his next day's duties vivid lines kept recurring to him

> A litle lowly hermitage it was,
> Downe in a dale . . .

Spenser used everything for his effects: consonants, vowels, meter, rhymes.

> But full of fire and greedy hardiment
> The youthfull knight could not for ought be staide ...

Keats raced through *The Faerie Queene*, Clarke told someone later, "as a young horse through a spring meadow—
ramping!"

He ramped through Spenserian imagery, noted the distillation that Spenser made from his own classic knowledge:

> Now when the rosy fingred Morning faire ...

through the gaudy figures of speech:

> As a tall ship tossed in troublous seas ...

through the allegory:

> Cruell Revenge, and rancorous Despight,
> Disloyall Treason, and hart-burning Hate ...

Keats cared little that Spenser was preaching the virtues
and championing the Church of England. It was Spenser the
poet who held up a "wonderous myrrhour" and in it Keats
saw an image of himself, an image of Keats the poet. Under
the spell of the Spenserian stanza—eight lines of iambic pentameter with a ninth line of hexameter, and the rhyme scheme
ababbcbcc—he found pen and paper and began an experiment
of his own, "Imitation of Spenser."

> Now Morning from her orient chamber came,
> And her first footsteps touch'd a verdant hill;
> Crowning its lawny crest with amber flame,
> Silv'ring the untainted gushes of its rill;
> Which, pure from mossy beds, did down distill,
> And after parting beds of simple flowers,
> By many streams a little lake did fill,
> Which round its marge reflected woven bowers,
> And, in its middle space, a sky that never lowers.

He managed to complete four stanzas and reread them, filled with the intoxication of achievement. He had turned a poem with his own hand! He'd show Clarke! No, no, he would not. He could show it to his brothers, though, when he went up to London to see them.

George and Tom lived at 4 Pancras Lane, in quarters over Abbey's warehouse, in the midst of all the commercial hurly-burly of the oldest section of London. All three brothers were lonely for one another and shared their news eagerly whenever they could rendezvous in town or at their grand-mother's.

John's poem was as much a miracle to them as to him, and they were as blissfully unaware as he that it was filled with forced rhymes and borrowed phrases.

"You have talent, John!" they said. "It is a fine poem. Do turn out some more."

That was encouragement enough for John to begin to think of himself as a poet and to send him delving more deeply into the craft. He gave up reading prose altogether.

Poetry was highly fashionable and becoming more so when John Keats was in his teens. The romantic revival was in its ascendancy, and Keats was ready for it. Romanticism urged the glorification of human emotions; John Keats was filled with adolescent emotions. The movement called for a return to nature; John Keats, boy of the fields, rivers, and hedgerows, had never left her. The reaction away from the rigid conventions of neoclassicism called for freedom of the imagination, and Keats's imagination was still too young to have suffered any enslavement to convention. A poet's imagination must be free to travel where it would, with the ancient Greek gods, through the forests and fields, out amongst the stars and planets, consorting with mythical creatures and real, in the past, the present, even the future. A tree could bleed; a man could converse with a butterfly, or marry a goddess.

The shadow of William Wordsworth fell across Keats's path very early. Wordsworth, high priest of the literary revolution, declared that the most commonplace thing could be rendered divine by the human imagination. Heading the revolt against artificial sophistications, Wordsworth took his following along country lanes, beside mountain-rimmed lakes, knelt before flowering plants, and declared that here was absolute integrity. They could trust nature. She would never betray them.

The poet, said Wordsworth, must seek an infinite variety of verse patterns in order to express himself; he must break away from the fixed metrical arrangements of the past generation. Poetry is the "real language of men in a state of vivid sensation." The poet must give his emotions free rein, must let his "heart leap up" whenever it would. The poet, although he will fail many times, must always strive to "produce upon all occasions language as exquisitely fitted for the passion as that which the real passion itself suggests." The poet sings "a song in which all human beings join him." Poetry is "the breath and finer spirit of all knowledge." Poetry is the "spontaneous overflow of powerful feelings; it takes its origin from emotion recollected in tranquillity."

Wordsworth published *The Excursion* in 1814, during Keats's third year of apprenticeship to Hammond, and by the time Keats read its commentaries on society his own rapidly deepening maturity was ready for its philosophic tenderness. Social protests and reforms were intimately related to the romantic movement in literature. While the young poets cried for freedom for man's spirit and emotions, the reformers called for freedom from poverty and oppression, and often both cries came from the same ardent voice.

Keats's friendship with Charles Cowden Clarke brought him into early touch with the whole liberal movement. He not only borrowed books from Clarke, but the liberal periodicals to which he subscribed, and he began to mingle with Clarke's circle of intellectual friends.

The Examiner, a Sunday paper, was one of the liberal periodicals that touched both Keats and Clarke closely. *The Examiner's* pages, as many as sixteen of them to an issue, were about seven inches wide by nine and three-quarters long, divided into two columns, and its opening columns "examined" political matters. Next came "Foreign Intelligence," then "Provincial Intelligence" tinged with gossip, then theatrical and literary news and comment, followed by a specialized and often continued article on a social abuse. *The Examiner* had a remarkably large circulation because its news reporting was highly accurate, and it was popular all over the British Isles. The publisher's young brother, James Henry Leigh Hunt, who wrote literary criticisms for it, was a friend of Clarke's, and Keats learned to admire Leigh Hunt long before he met him.

In his borrowed copies of *The Examiner* Keats learned of the artistic times in which he lived. He read of Mrs. Siddons and John Philip Kemble, of the paintings of Benjamin West, and the young Benjamin Robert Haydon. He read reviews of the works of Wordsworth, Coleridge, Sir Walter Scott, Maria Edgeworth, and Lord Byron. Hunt particularly admired Byron. In *The Examiner* Keats read articles by Charles Lamb, and a vivid protest against the choice of Robert Southey as Poet Laureate.

Often Keats and Clarke read the newly arrived *Examiner* together, and drew a quiet thrill from the courage of the Hunt brothers, who had already been prosecuted for exposing such scandalous government matters as intolerable conditions in the army, or the shocking personal life and character of the Prince Regent. Time and again *The Examiner* attacked the Tory administration; in 1811, the year in which Keats had begun his apprenticeship to Hammond, Leigh Hunt and his brother had been arrested and charged with seditious libel for calling the Prince Regent "a rake and a liar." They had made an impassioned plea and had been acquitted, but the subject continued to be debated in competing periodicals.

His personal excitement over watching for each issue of the Hunt publication kindled in Keats a fervor for human freedom; even though he never became personally active in politics, he entered the camp of the liberals to stay. In one of the issues for March 1812, the Regent was referred to as a "violator of his word, a libertine over head and ears in debt and disgrace, a despiser of domestic ties, the companion of gamblers . . ." and the article brought the case back into the courtroom where the Hunts were charged once more with libel. This time they were indicted and sent to prison for two years, and Leigh Hunt's martyrdom for freedom of expression was a part of John Keats's maturing.

Keats helped Clarke pack periodic baskets of fruit and vegetables and eggs to take to Leigh Hunt in prison and waited eagerly for Clarke to return from his visit to the prison to tell him what he had seen. Was it particularly awful? Was Leigh Hunt suffering quite badly? Well, no, it was not really too bad, Clarke reported, although the two brothers were in different prisons. Leigh Hunt was in Surrey Gaol, and he was soon permitted to have his wife and children with him—and visitors—and his pianoforte and library. He was continuing to issue *The Examiner* from prison. Prominent literary figures began to beat a path to Surrey, and Clarke came back to Enfield to report with much animation that Lord Byron had made a personal call upon Hunt.

Byron! Keats had already read the first two cantos of *Childe Harold's Pilgrimage*. Lord Byron was only in his early twenties, and *Childe Harold* was his first serious work. Before its publication Byron had been an unknown; afterward he was the rage of the literary and social world. Keats rushed with everyone else to read *The Gaiour* and *The Bride of*

Abydos when they came out. Byron sent complimentary
copies of his new works to Hunt in prison. Hunt knew
Byron; Clarke knew Hunt; Keats knew Clarke. Could such
a circle ever close?

Keats studied Byron's rhyme patterns, the variations in his
rhythms. In *Childe Harold* he used iambic pentameter, and
in the first Turkish tale, *The Gaiour*, iambic tetrameter and
rhymed couplets; but in *Abydos* he began with dactylic to
announce the scene and settled back into iambic couplets for
the narrative. He was no slave to a convention even when
he set it up himself!

> Byron! how sweetly sad thy melody!

And Keats seized a pen once more and began another
poem: his sonnet to Byron.

> Attuning still the soul to tenderness,
> As if soft Pity, with unusual stress,
> Had touch'd her plaintive lute, and thou, being by,
> Hadst caught the tones, nor suffer'd them to die.

Poetry did not come easily; Keats felt his lack of experience. *Melody* had to rhyme with *by;* though he would have
liked it to be better. The seventh line had only four measures
instead of five; the best he could do with his hero's bright
halo was to let it shine *beamily;* and the only bird that
would fit the meter of the thirteenth line was a *dying swan.*
But the thought of the sonnet, "To Byron," was clear and
authentic. Byron did sing to a "plaintive lute," and his talent
was filtered through private sorrow:

> As when a cloud the golden moon doth veil,
> Its sides are ting'd with a resplendent glow . . .

Byron! How sweetly sad! How delicious vicarious sorrow
can be! How enchanting his "tale of pleasing woe."

Keats laid down his pen, rose with weary self-satisfaction at having finished his sonnet, walked to his washstand and studied himself in the mirror. He tried a sweet-sad smile and liked the effect. Then he unwound and removed the stock tie and laid the collar of his shirt open at the throat. Yes, his neck was smooth enough for the style. His forehead was high enough, though not too high, his mouth sensitive and moderately sensuous. His reddish-brown hair waved about his ears becomingly, and his hazel-brown eyes were large and expressive. Oh, yes! He could play the poet's role.

CHAPTER IV

O Solitude!

HIS POET'S ROLE and his poet's vocation were nurtured in ways that Byron could have envied. John Keats's early sorrows were of the ripening and deepening kind, and there was always an aura of love, genuine admiration, respect, and encouragement about him. The circle of his immediate family dwindled over the years, but he was never robbed of it abruptly, and when a family member was removed there was usually an intimate friend to fill the vacancy.

From the first line of verse that he wrote, Tom and George were thrilled and amazed to have a genius for a brother, and in each new poem that he took to them they saw his progress and struggling growth. Even his grandmother, though she would have preferred a more substantial career for him, treated the "young horse" with cautious affection.

On holidays, when the two apprentices came home from London, the four of them could gather around the dining-room table with their grandmother in her black presiding as

40

of old. John was developing into a most able talker, and with his rapidly accumulating reading knowledge he dominated the table from his corner and grew stronger in his role of head of the house. It gave him a secret twinge of alarm to reflect that his grandmother was looking frail and what her loss would mean to all of them. In 1814 she was 78, and they could not hope to have her forever. Toward the end of that same year she fell ill.

Poet and doctor in Keats lived in very close kinship; each possessed tenderness and compassion; each reached out for spiritual fellowship; each responded with acute sensitiveness to human need and suffering. But John Keats at nineteen was less able to assume direction of the family and his stricken grandmother than he had at fourteen because of the frustrating—and legal—presence of Abbey. Richard and Eleanor Abbey arrived with dispatch, and Mrs. Abbey swept Fanny into her care.

"She will, of course, go back to Walthamstow with us. I think Miss Tuckey's school would be a fine one for her."

The Abbeys had two residences, one in Pancras Lane in London for the winter, and a second in the suburban village of Walthamstow, where they spent their summers.

Mr. Abbey sent the three brothers back to their apprenticeships and provided for Mrs. Jennings's care. Heated and resentful protests from John and Tom were spent upon the air. Only George saw the reason and good intent in Abbey's decisions about themselves and Fanny, but he could not soften anyone's attitude.

"He is quite tactless and his wife is an ignorant gabbler," George agreed, "but he's a responsible fellow, I think, with a big task handling such a difficult lot as we."

"I'm not so difficult for Abbey as I hope to be some day," said John darkly, even though he knew the threat was an idle one.

Abbey had ridiculed some of his poetry recently, and he still smarted from it.

Mrs. Jennings's illness was not a protracted one, and she sank gradually into death. On December 19, 1814, another dreary caravan set out for London to bury her at St. Stephen's, Coleman Street.

Gloom settled slowly around John Keats once more like a lowering black cloud as he returned to his room in Dr. Hammond's cottage. There could be no more walking up Church Street to his grandmother's, no more jovial sessions around her dining table. The house would pass to the hands of strangers. Fanny was to remain permanently with the Abbeys, and his brothers were in London. There was no one here any more except Charles Clarke, two miles away, and the stupid Hammond. Death had wrought this further change, as it had wrought every other before it.

Death, mused Keats in his sudden solitude, was a destroyer of family patterns, a humbler of the living. He did not want to study his poet's features in the mirror this day. He could look at any part of his flesh to know that death had not touched it. Yet, death was a rescuer of the stricken. The soul released could start up and away, freed of its sufferings. To where?

> As from the darkening gloom a silver dove
> Upsoars, and darts into the Eastern light,
> On pinions that naught moves but pure delight,
> So fled thy soul into the realms above,
> Regions of peace and everlasting love . . .

There *must* be a divine realm! Souls that he had known, that lived so acutely in his own memory, must be going on somewhere. What other justification for grief could there be?

Wherefore does any grief our joy impair?

There were no missing meters in his sonnet on death and only one strained rhyme: *love* and *prove;* and its universal theme, seeking the forbidden answer to the eternal riddle, had come from deeper levels within himself. Knowing this, candidily realizing it as he reread the finished poem, Keats's own spirit soared upward out of its gloom.

He did not share this poem with anyone immediately. This poem on death was intimate, still too warm to expose, and as he resumed his rounds with Hammond he continued to turn it over in his mind and enjoy it. Hammond rebuked him for his absent-mindedness, and the sudden intrusion upon his secret thoughts brought Keats's hot temper flaring up. Words were exchanged. He shook his fist in the doctor's face.

Keats and Hammond had had many differences, and this one blew over like the others, but the rebuke had done no good. Keats merely walked in the doctor's world and lived in his own, waiting for the end of the day so that he could spend what remained of it with Clarke.

One afternoon Clarke greeted him with the good news that Leigh Hunt had been released from prison.

Their champion, freedom's martyr, their most enlightened literary critic, was at liberty, his two-year sentence completed. This was exciting news for all the young radicals. Leigh Hunt had lived up to the best tradition in intellectual prisoners, had even published that volume of poems-written-while-in-prison and had composed part of a long narrative poem, *The Story of Rimini*, with much encouragement from Lord Byron. To Keats, Leigh Hunt was a great spirit who grew greater in suffering, one who ignored his prison walls and roamed abroad with Spenser and Milton. During all of Hunt's imprisonment, Keats wrote, "his immortal spirit had been as free as the sky-searching lark."

Keats wrote his sonnet, "Written on the Day That Mr. Leigh Hunt Left Prison," that same night, and when he reread it next morning he was frankly pleased. Its rhymes were true, and its lines reasonably smooth, and only after he had grown well beyond it would he be able to look back and realize the triteness of its language. Now, on this crisp February morning of 1815, it told him that his poet's resources were richer than he had had any idea, that he needed only the gentle touch of an idea, a single inspiring fact or experience, to bring forth a deluge of metrical language.

He decided to risk showing this poem to Clarke, and on his next free afternoon he started out toward Enfield. But about midway he met Clarke walking toward Edmonton and so he turned around and they walked together.

"I am going up to London," Clarke told him, "to see Leigh Hunt and pay my respects to him and his family."

Going to see Leigh Hunt! Keats's pulse went up visibly and his cheeks turned a little pink at the idea.

"Would you like to meet him?" asked Clarke.

Keats's pulse rushed higher, and he fingered the piece of paper in his pocket.

"I must introduce you some day," Clarke promised as they paused at a field-gate where Clarke would turn off toward London.

After a brief moment of self-conscious indecision Keats handed Clarke the sonnet on Leigh Hunt, and stood breathing hard as his friend read it. Now Clarke knew! Now Clarke knew what his vocation must be, knew how much his teaching and friendship and reading-companionship meant. Charles Clarke's face was sober as he concluded the last line and slipped the sonnet into his own pocket.

"It is a well-turned piece, John."

Clarke went on to London and Keats hurried back to the Hammond cottage. A well-turned piece! A well-turned piece! There would be better-turned pieces, and better, and better, and better. He would work and work, improve his skills, learn, increase his vocabulary, experiment with verse forms. He would expose himself to every inspiration, on the printed page, in life, so that those deep unknown resources could all in time be prodded free.

In a very few days he had written two more poems, one an eight-stanza piece "To Hope" and the other an "Ode to Apollo." In the former he dropped the sonnet form but clung to the iambic pentameter, and in the ode he worked cautiously with the trochaic foot and varying line lengths. In among the platitudes bright spots were beginning to appear: "Homer with his nervous arms" and "expectant stand the spheres"; but they were almost lost among such threadbare expressions as "trumpets sound afar."

To the young man who now knew himself to be a writer, the name of Leigh Hunt became a bright symbol, and Keats listened eagerly to news of him: Hunt and his wife and children took lodgings in Edgeware Road until his health could recover from the two-year confinement; his brother lived very nearby; Lord Byron continued to visit Hunt; Hunt said that Byron's appearance was the finest he had ever seen it, elegant, gentlemanly, "the turn of his head and countenance have a spirit of elevation"; Wordsworth paid Hunt a call, exchanged thoughts with him on present-day poets; Byron was quite jealous of the fact that Hunt had called Wordsworth "the prince of the bards of his time."

News of this fabulous and nebulous other world of contemporary poets created for Keats the dream in which he could walk and into which he could retreat from his rapidly growing distaste for Hammond and the village from which his entire family had departed. When Clarke's parents began to talk of giving up the school in Enfield and leaving the region, Keats wondered in panic what he would do if Charles moved away.

Toward the end of the summer he had it out with Abbey.

He was sick of the doddering Hammond, sick of forsaken Church Street, sick of his rural apprenticeship, sick of his little room up over the laboratory! His brothers were in London. Why could he not go up to London to study medicine near them? The cost would come out of income earned by his own funds; Abbey could scarcely suffer from the change. All Abbey had to do was make the arrangements and persuade Hammond to break the contract of apprenticeship. Abbey did consent, and even though the apprenticeship had another year to run, so did Hammond, with a readiness that indicated they were both willing to see the belligerent young hothead happy elsewhere. Before the end of September nineteen-year-old John Keats was on the road to London, headed for a gay reunion with his brothers. Even though they could not all live together, they were going to be closer than they had been in nearly four years. John's room was at 8 Dean Street, on the south side of the Thames, within two blocks of Guy's Hospital where he was to study, within easy walking distance of Pancras Lane.

John was particularly glad that he could keep a closer eye on Tom, because Tom's health was not good. At sixteen Tom ought to be more robust; he was wan, underweight, and sometimes John saw in his eyes something that reminded him of his mother. Eighteen-year-old George, on the other hand, seemed built to endure. John Keats—still the oldest, still head of the family—decided that he would pay a visit to twelve-year-old Fanny as soon as possible. Walthamstow was much more convenient to him now.

He enrolled in the medical school of Guy's Hospital on the first of October, 1815, for a course of training far more rigorous and testing than his apprenticeship to a country doctor had been. Keats, with a group of boys, was assigned to one of the hospital surgeons, a Dr. William Lucas, and part of their training was to walk the wards twice a week with the doctor. The rest of the training would be to attend lectures, sometimes watch operations in the theater of St. Thomas's Hospital across the street, and dissect cadavers in the "dead-house."

His excitement at being so close to the realities of his future profession swept all other interests aside for the time being.

"Tell me about Lucas," he asked a more advanced student. "Is he a brilliant doctor?"

The upperclassman laughed derisively at the suggestion. "He's a frightful old bungler," he replied. "Deaf as a post and awkward about everything he does. I hope you get a chance to watch Astley Cooper. There is a real surgeon!"

The name of the famous Astley Cooper was as fabulous to Keats as the names of Hunt, Bryon, and Wordsworth, and he heard it frequently as he hurried along the corridor with the crowd of laughing, gabbing, joking students after the shuffling, bent figure of Lucas. They followed the surgeon into a ward and crowded around the bed of a patient to watch as Lucas and his "dresser" or assistant examined a wound and changed its dressings. Keats's heart constricted and his stomach turned nauseous at the sight of the swollen, purple, proud flesh around the area of the incision. Keats knew what the patient's fate must be. After the desperate courage spent in living through an operation with crude instruments and no anesthetic, he must die of the subsequent infection.

His fellow students jostled and jogged the bed, oblivious of the patient's pain and embarrassment. Keats's first patient had been his mother; he took only one look at this patient's eyes and did not look again.

But in the dissecting room, where they investigated bones, muscles, and nerves, the bodies delivered to the students by professional grave robbers could feel no pain, and there was

no danger in looking at the eyes. The raucousness of the
young men was an obvious bravado, part of the necessary
hardening of a doctor's moral fiber.

The initial excitement over this experience in a new kind
of world faded quickly. From the coarseness and cruelty of
the hospital wards Keats returned to the solitude of his room,
his mind filled with distasteful memories of foul odors, blood-
stained dressings, and soiled bedding, to look out of his
window upon the squalid slums of the district. Books, studies,
the printed word, the written word, formed the only screen
behind which he could retreat. He read and he wrote. He
read Leigh Hunt's *Rimini* as soon as he could obtain a copy,
ramping through the fresh greenness, the gentle rains at
night, cottage trees, bubbling springs, singing birds, horses
whose "bridles glance about with gold and gems," mulberry
and bay, pines, pools and rushes, "wild pear and oak and dusky
juniper," and every reference to the unspoiled natural out-of-
doors that he had lost by coming to London. He reveled in
the saccharine romance of Francesca and Paolo. The old
Italian tale was tenderly tragic; it told of unfulfilled love
frustrated by death—death of the lover brought about by the
avenging husband, death of the lady brought about by her
grief and shock.

During his solitary hours in Dean Street, John Keats began
to write the early faint beginnings of his extraordinary other
literary achievement, his letters. At first it did not occur to
him to separate his conversations-by-mail from his verse
writing.

> Sweet are the pleasures that to verse belong,
> And doubly sweet a brotherhood in song;
> Nor can remembrance, Mathew! bring to view
> A fate more pleasing, a delight more true
> Than that in which the brother Poets joy'd . . .

The Mathew of this long verse epistle was George Felton Mathew, a friend of Tom's and George's. Mathew and his sister and parents lived in an ample and hospitable home in the Regent's Park section of London, and they entertained many of London's young literary set. As soon as the Mathews learned from Tom and George of their talented older brother, John was included in their gatherings, and the occasional exposures to their warmth went a long way to ease his loneliness.

Keats soon learned that Leigh Hunt and his family had moved to Hampstead Heath in a section called Vale of Health just north of Regent's Park, and he hoped that someday the currents of literary life would draw him into that salon as well.

The happiest balm to his solitude was the arrival of Charles Cowden Clarke in London. The elder Clarkes had carried out their plan to give up the school, and when they left Enfield Charles moved in with his sister Isabella and brother-in-law, John Towers, a chemist, in 6 Little Warner Street, Clerkenwell, on the north edge of London, and within walking distance of Guy's Hospital—walking distance, that is, for a young man with a healthy stride accustomed to walking. From the very short Dean Street Keats could turn left into Tooley Street, then right over London Bridge to the north side of the Thames and choose several routes northwestward to Little Warner Street. Pancras Lane where his brothers lived lay on the best route, and so did St. Paul's Cathedral and Christ's Hospital.

What a joy to sit and talk with Clarke once more! He could describe to Charles the beastly section he was living in, full of "dirt, turnings, and windings," and show him his latest poems. The two young men, no longer teacher and student, were reunited in a torrent of conversation, a flood tide of idealism.

Through the Mathews and Clarke John Keats became known to the artistic young set in London, and rapidly gained a position of prominence and popularity. He brought vigor and ardor into the room with him, a cheerful and ready wit, a fresh-air glow in spite of the murky city atmosphere in which he now lived, and a naturalist's knowledge of things wild. He spoke fluently and from his excellent memory could call up at will favorite passages and appropriate lines. His conversations—almost monologues at times—were a distillation of everything he read as though reading and breathing were identical processes, each adding its own kind of oxygen to his blood.

Keats shared his own resources with generous abandon. To him poets were a kind of supermen, and all artists were a peg above the rest of mankind. They must feed mankind from their magical fountains. His own faith in the arts was unshakable, and when he met a young painter named Joseph Severn who was suffering from discouragement Keats rushed to envelop him in energy.

Severn, he discovered, was a warm-hearted, shy, rather naïve fellow, two years older than himself, battling both family and poverty for his right to be a painter. His father had forced him into apprenticeship to an engraver for eight years, but he had stubbornly found time to study at the Royal Academy. When he and Keats met, Severn was almost free of his apprenticeship and eking out a living by painting miniature portraits. Keats lifted him out of his despondency by his own natural eagerness to learn about yet another art—painting. What was it? What were its techniques? Severn's background was just as limited in books, and he marveled at how much Keats had read. Keats discoursed with him at length about Spenser and Shakespeare and Milton, urged a copy of *A Midsummer Night's Dream* upon him, read him passages from *The Faerie Queene*.

"You have raised me to the third heaven," Severn told Keats.

Another time they went walking together in the country, and Severn was amazed at Keats's powers of observation.

"We haven't missed the note of a bird, the rustle of an animal in the hedges, or the coloring of a single flower," he said.

Keats played his poet's role well in his ardent Byronic way, his collar open at the neck, his sensitive face a study in subtlety, an other-world expression in his eyes. He grew more and more popular socially and soon acquired a small bevy of feminine admirers. George Felton Mathew's two young cousins, Caroline and Anne Mathew, and his sister Mary, adored Keats in the best romantic drawing-room manner. Mary copied his verses into her personal album, and Caroline and Anne sent him suitable mementos, one time a sentimental poem by the Irish poet, Thomas Moore, and a "curious shell," which he acknowledged in extravagant verse:

> Hast thou from the caves of Golconda, a gem
>   Pure as the ice-drop that froze on the mountain?
> Bright as the humming-bird's green diadem,
>   When it flutters in sun-beams that shine through a fountain?

The pulses and daydreams of other young ladies were beginning to be affected by John Keats, for one sent him—anonymously—a laurel wreath long before his poetry showed enough promise to justify it. The result was another early Keats sonnet.

John Keats's youngest feminine admirer was his sister. After a few weeks of orientation in London he hurried out to Walthamstow to pay her a visit in the parlor of the genteel and chilly "Ladies Boarding Academy" run by the Misses Mary and Susanna Tuckey. Twelve-year-old Fanny rushed to her brother and clung to him, shivering, as though he had come as her rescuing knight. She was lonely for him and George and Tom! And living with the Abbeys was dreadful! Were they cruel? he demanded to know. No, not cruel, just strict; and so senseless. They never read books! They didn't care two sticks about things like books or music or poetry. He wanted to know about her school, and she assured him that she liked the school and the other girls there. She thanked heaven it was a boarding school, and she only had to be at home with the Abbeys on holidays.

John knew what his sister meant. The Abbeys were substantial, and their house of red brick was handsome enough and well supplied with domestic help; but there was nothing in it to strike a spark in a keen young imagination. The Abbeys were soulless vegetables, he agreed.

He felt her arms and fingered the texture of her dress. She was too thin, and she ought to wear warmer clothing.

"No wonder you take cold so often," he reproached her.

She promised to be more careful. And would he come to see her whenever he could? Yes, yes, he promised.

He walked back into town in a cloud of depression. Both Fanny and Tom were sickly, and he must watch over them carefully. Oh, why could they not all be together—the four of them! Why need there be any guardianship?

When he crossed the Thames into the slums on its southern side, his mood grew still darker. There at the top of the stairs was his dreary little room where he must pass so many hours in solitude if he was to accomplish any studying and reading and writing. Solitude! He flung himself upon the bed and closed his eyes, conjuring up happy visions of golden fields and cloudless blue skies.

Still steeped in his poetic images, he walked to his lecture hall next morning and sat among the large audience of young men. He spread his notebook out before him and tried earnestly to listen to the droning voice of the lecturer. In a small, crowded handwriting he took down information about the blood—its temperature, its red corpuscles, theories on the cause of its clotting.

In those early days of the nineteenth century modern medicine had already emerged a long way out of superstition and ignorance, but the road ahead of it was still long. Pathology was a science; circulation of the blood was known; the red blood corpuscles had recently been discovered; comparative anatomy was an established concept; doctors were beginning to understand such body chemical processes as digestion; vaccination against smallpox with cowpox vaccine had been discovered; castor oil, cod-liver oil, and digitalis were in general use; microorganisms were observed in the crude microscopes of the times. But antisepsis was far in the future, and Keats would never hear the names of Pasteur, Lister, and Koch.

When Keats was a medical student, treatment through mesmerism was a subject of much bantering and play-acting among the young men; and when they heard the rumors of a new instrument called a stethoscope, they laughed coarsely and declared they much preferred to lay their heads against a lady's bosom and grope about for her heart. Many vowed they would make professional calls only on families wealthy enough to have water closets in their houses.

Keats grinned with the others at the vulgar banter, since ladies' bosoms were as intriguing to a poet as to a doctor. Yet his fellow students were never more than half-phantoms to him—nor friends, nor enemies, simply lads with whom he did not make much personal contact and from whom he dashed to his literary soirees when his class hours were over.

The contents of the lectures progressed. Keats learned the bones of the body and the fixed arrangements of muscles. The world of dreams held him to no such fixed arrangements as the bones and the muscles. Out of the window of the lecture hall and beyond were glimpses of white clouds traveling across a blue sky, the same sky that formed a ceiling over the natural world of meadow and birds, hedgerow and flowers. He pulled a pencil out of his pocket and began to draw flowers in the margin of his notebook.

"The lecture is finished, Keats," someone told him, and he got up to leave the room with the others.

Sometimes the lectures were genuinely dull and then to amuse himself and his fellow students he wrote verse in the notebook of the man sitting next to him:

> Give me women, wine and snuff
> Until I cry out, "hold! enough!"
> You may do so sans objection
> Till the day of resurrection;
> For bless my beard they aye shall be
> My beloved Trinity.

But there were some lectures that could hold his attention throughout. He was lucky enough, after all, to be able to hear the great Astley Cooper. Sir Astley was striking, an effective speaker, a brilliant doctor, and when he lectured on the physiology of the nervous system or surgical techniques, only the sick stayed away. Cooper was sensitive enough to be stirred by what he saw in the eyes of a patient, and wept at the thought of having to inflict pain on a child. He looked out over the nearly three hundred faces in the lecture theater and noted one in particular—the dream-laden face of John Keats. Keats, staring directly at Cooper while the man talked and only half seeing him, was suddenly startled to realize that Cooper was actually trying to catch his eye.

"Stop by at the end of the hour."

Keats nodded, and at the close of the session tarried by Dr. Cooper's table, feeling quite small beside the towering surgeon.

"I should like to see you with me in the wards tomorrow, Keats."

There was undiluted inspiration in receiving personal at-

tention from the prominent and brilliant doctor, and John
Keats, rendered momentarily on fire for medicine, appeared
with the eager crowd of young men to watch the surgeon
work and listen to his comments as he went from bed to
bed. Dr. Cooper's assistant or "dresser" was a personal rela-
tive, George Cooper, who carried a tin box of supplies,
changed dressings on wounds and rendered other services to
the patients at the attending surgeon's instructions.

But even under Sir Astley's guidance the wounds turned
purple and swollen, the bandages were just as bloody, the
linens just as soiled; and by the time Keats had returned to
his own quarters, the pendulum of his mood swung back to
the other extreme, and the sudden enthusiasm induced by the
cordiality of the Coopers was rapidly replaced by an attack
of acute loneliness.

The only companion who never deserted him was his "coy
muse," and to shut out the "murky" gloom of his "beastly
place" he took up his pen and began to work on a poem.

> O Solitude! if I must with thee dwell,
>   Let it not be among the jumbled heap
>   Of murky buildings; climb with me the steep,—
> Nature's observatory—whence the dell,
> Its flowery slopes, its river's crystal swell,
>   May seem a span . . .

A poem is something felt, Wordsworth had said.

>   . . . let me thy vigils keep
>   'Mongst boughs pavilion'd, where the deer's swift leap
> Startles the wild bee from the fox-glove bell.

Poetry is the "real language of men in a state of vivid sensation."

> But though I'll gladly trace these scenes with thee,
>   Yet the sweet converse of an innocent mind,

Whose words are images of thoughts refin'd,
    Is my soul's pleasure . . .

"Poetry is the breath and finer spirit of all knowledge."

                                    . . . and it sure must be
    Almost the highest bliss of human-kind,
        When to thy haunts two kindred spirits flee.

Poetry is the "spontaneous overflow of powerful feelings; it takes its origin from emotion recollected in tranquillity."

The thought completed, the last line of the sonnet accomplished, the poet's energy vanished, his head nodded, and he fell asleep across his writing table.

But one sonnet, no matter how well turned, could not banish his loneliness for more than a night, and Dr. Cooper, as soon as he became aware of what he thought was the problem, recommended a solution. Perhaps, thought the sensitive teacher, if Keats was less lonely he would take more interest in his medicine, and so it was arranged that Keats move around the corner to St. Thomas Street and share rooms with George Cooper and two other lads. The four young men were sufficiently companionable and their medical studies gave them a community of interest; but to a poet the twin problem to a loathing of solitude was the need of solitary retirement in which to create. He could achieve that retirement only by withdrawing to himself in a corner of the room.

Gradually young Cooper did begin to understand that he was rooming with a poet, especially when the poet's brothers paid them a call and he saw the deep homage and wide-eyed admiration they paid to John. Tom and George knew that John would walk among the great some day; so far as they were concerned he already did.

The elder Cooper still saw a sensitive and compassionate doctor in the making, and he selected John Keats to be one of his dressers. The early advancement did win him back to a degree. Now and again a surgical wound did throw off its pus and heal cleanly; and there were human hearts stout enough to absorb the shock of the crude techniques. John Keats earnestly attended patients at Dr. Cooper's side and did still earnestly struggle to reconcile the dual compulsions of human service and art; but each poem that he wrote showed even to himself his rapid growth in language skill and increasing depth of thought, and as his sympathetic fingers unwound a bandage it was his poet's heart that responded to the suffering.

At the end of the term George Cooper and another of Keats's roommates completed their studies and left, and Keats continued to room with the third man, Henry Stephens, and a George Mackereth. Stephens had long since fallen under the spell of Keats's charm, and he was learning to judge and enjoy good poetry. He had become accustomed to having Keats suddenly interrupt his studying with a line of original verse and a, "What do you think?"

One evening Keats wheeled around in his chair and asked Stephens what he thought of the line:

A thing of beauty is a constant joy.

"It has the true ring, but is wanting in some way," was Stephens's reply.

Keats lapsed into a long silence and finally read another line to Stephens:

A thing of beauty is a joy forever.

"That will live forever," Stephens assured him.

Keats kept the line on a scrap of paper and added no more to it then, and for a while it slipped from his awareness, although the experience of producing it had added its bit to the medicine versus poetry conflict.

He told Charles Cowden Clarke more than once of his

fading interest in his medical studies when he visited him in Clerkenwell.

"I am no physician, Charles. The other day during the lecture, there came a sunbeam into the room, and with it a whole troop of creatures floating in the ray; and I was off with them to Oberon and fairyland."

Clarke could not help but smile in the warmest and most understanding way.

"What have you written lately?" he asked, and Keats gave him a copy of the sonnet, "O Solitude."

Week after week Keats put off the decision that was growing upon him. Week after week the substance of the lectures and the company of his roommates grew more remote, and he hurried from them to the company of artists. Every reading hour that could be spared from study requirements was spent in consuming poetry. He began to learn correct pronunciation of Greek proper names so that he could rhyme them precisely.

"I have something to show you," Clarke told him one May evening, and he handed John Keats the brand new May 5, 1816, issue of *The Examiner*.

Clarke would not make such an incident of it unless the paper really contained something extraordinary. Keats found a chair and began to turn the pages until his eye lighted on it in the lower right-hand corner of page 282—a group of shortened, unreconciled lines—*O Solitude! if I must with thee dwell*—HIS POEM—accepted for publication. O Poetry! since I must with thee dwell, hold sweet converse with thy imagery, sing high hymns to thy harmonies, court thy diverse passions . . .

He looked up into Clarke's face and saw a humble, gentle, happy smile. Teacher! Friend! Mentor! Guide!

"You gave it to him, Charles?"

Clarke sat down beside him quickly and related his conversations with Hunt.

"Just recently I was spending an evening with Leigh Hunt out at Vale of Health and took the opportunity to show him some more of your poems, since he had liked 'O Solitude.' "

"Which ones did you give him?" Keats interrupted eagerly.

"I showed him 'How Many Bards,' your sonnet to him, and one or two others, 'Calidore,' I think, and 'Induction to a Poem.' He read them aloud and I was simply unprepared for his unhesitating and prompt admiration."

"Which one did he like best?"

"Oh, 'Bards.' A fellow critic named Horace Smith was there, and when Hunt read the 'Bards,' Smith particularly liked the last six lines and repeated the line, *That distance of recognizance bereaves,* and clapped his hands in applause, calling it a well condensed expression."

John Keats, lips parted to ease his breathing, watched every expression of Clarke's face lest he miss a single word he was being told.

"They asked all sorts of questions about you after that, and they were quite startled when I told them you had not yet reached your majority. Here is the greatest treat of all, John. Leigh Hunt has requested me to bring you to him. He very particularly wants to meet you."

At long last it was coming true, the promise that Charles had made him more than a year ago.

"We will make a morning call," said Clarke, "Hunt will like that."

On that memorable morning they walked the whole distance. Keats set out from St. Thomas Street, stopped at Clarke's door in Clerkenwell, and together they took the road to Hampstead Heath.

The lusty, excitable Keats talked almost continuously as they matched their strides on the country road. Now and again Clarke was able to insert a thought or a word, but he did not struggle against the impossible. Keats was oblivious to the impression that he made on passersby, who turned whether on foot or mounted for a second glance at the young face animated to the point of beauty.

When Hampstead Village came into sight, John Keats turned suddenly silent and quickened his pace. The Vale of Health was gently rolling open country, and the two-story cottage stood among a green abundance of trees and laurel. The cottage was small and modest because large fines levied at the time of his conviction had reduced Hunt's circumstances severely. Hunt himself called the place a "packing box."

At the door of the house John Keats clasped the long, slim hand of a tall, slim man, and looked up into a dark-complexioned face with a rather voluptuous mouth, bright black eyes and jet black hair that grew well down on his forehead and hung almost into his eyes. He discovered Hunt's personality to be what others had described: witty, mischievous, occasionally a tease, warm and light-hearted; yet beneath the gay exterior lay the far-sighted idealism and love of mankind. Only thirty-two, Leigh Hunt could easily feel a compassion for young men just beginning to develop into creative artists, and he had an acute instinct for detecting real promise, particularly in poets.

Hunt opened his heart to Keats at once, and John Keats knew it. His first interview with Hunt developed into a whole morning's conversation, and the first morning proved not enough. John Keats returned to Vale of Health for two more "morning calls," in that tiny, low-ceilinged living room lined with books, and after that the door was always open to him. He had found a second home in his beloved rural countryside, had become a member of one of the most alive and stimulating salons in England, and had acquired a literary champion. He walked often to the Vale of Health, became friendly with Marianne Hunt, who sometimes let her house-keeping slide while she pursued her own talent for sculpture, and he played with the Hunts' small children, the oldest a boy of six, the youngest an infant girl who had been born during Hunt's imprisonment. Most enjoyable of all, he spent hours talking with Leigh Hunt.

"The sonnet is probably Italian in origin," Hunt told him. "It has a strict metrical pattern because in olden times it was recited to musical accompaniment. A sonnet must express a single thought—clearly—its lines must flow smoothly with no adjustments or words out of place, and its rhymes must be perfect and true."

It was not that John Keats did not know this by now, nor that Hunt thought he did not, but spoken by so excellent a critic it acquired particular authenticity.

"Shelley is a young man you ought to know," said Hunt. "I must bring you together some time."

Who was Shelley? A young poet like himself, Hunt explained. Shelley was probably twenty-three or twenty-four, had just published a long poem called *Alastor*. Hunt predicted a great future for him.

"His style is quite different from yours, Keats."

Hunt liked what he called "rustic walks," and sometimes Keats was lucky enough to be his companion along the wooded paths of Hampstead, perhaps even to linger with him at an inn and go on talking over a lamb chop, a salad, a cold gooseberry tart; or glance back from the elevation of the Heath at the view of London and St. Paul's.

Keats still had not resolved his decision on medicine as a career, and on July 25, 1816, he went up for an interim examination, an oral test to determine his qualifications as an apothecary. He justified Astley Cooper's confidence in him by passing and receiving a certificate that permitted him to practice as an apothecary—to prescribe, prepare, administer, and even sell medicines and pills.

The certificate from the Examiners of the Society of Apothecaries was a major step toward becoming a physician, and a young man coming out of the dark corridors of St. Thomas's into the bright square courtyard could finger the scroll in his hand with deep satisfaction. Only a lad who felt the call of a real vocation could have come this far with it; and John Keats, walking across the cobblestoned enclosure and out through the iron gates to the street on that warm summer day, did feel some leaning to medicine. But he was also compelled by a stronger vocation, and his apothecary's certificate was a milestone standing at the point where the road of his career divided and the two compulsions became distinct and separate.

Poetry *was* a calling, entirely possible in an era when poetry had such a vogue. Keats had been thinking all this time of the greats, those who were established—Wordsworth, Byron, and before them Spenser, Shakespeare. They'd once been unknown young men. Who was Shelley? No one knew, yet Shelley had thrown in his lot with poetry, and Hunt thought Shelley would succeed some day. Hunt thought it of John Keats too! And Hunt *knew*, Keats thought fervently; he *knew*. His decision developed within him like a rapidly gathering whirlwind, carried him across the river to Pancras Lane, and he burst into his brothers' quarters like a gust of wind.

"I've decided it!" he declared.

Decided what? That he would give up his medical studies and devote himself to writing poetry! There was no lack of faith to be found in his brothers. With uproarious enthusiasm they cheered him on, and their voices filled the room, John's the deepest and richest of all.

"John Keats, toast of London!" declared George.

"John Keats, Poet Laureate of England!" shouted young Tom.

"I shall never be Poet Laureate," John laughed. "I have too many radical friends."

"Maybe you'll outlive this regime."

"Come! We shall celebrate."

Out of the house and into the street they stomped and strode happily across town to the Thames and over it to Southwark. There cheap wine could be purchased in decrepit-looking inns for even less than on the north side, and once having redoubled their energies they sought out an all-male hall where they could stamp, cheer, jeer, and shout around a bear-baiting arena.

Tom began to cough in the dust and stale air, and his brothers soon took him outside.

"It was—just—stuffiness and excitement—" he protested.

But John's professionally trained ear heard a chest condition, and he looked hard at George.

"He's had a touch of a cold," George admitted.

"At this time of year?"

"Oh, city air is always foul," said Tom, whose face suddenly seemed unnaturally white.

They started to walk back, holding to a slow pace so that Tom wouldn't have to breathe too hard.

"Are you all right now?" asked John, as they reached St. Thomas Street.

George and Tom both gave him every reassurance, and they parted company, John to his quarters with the two medical students, his brothers to Pancras Lane.

He was free, now, John realized, free to give more time and thought to his family. Tom needed some fresh country air. Then why not a holiday for Tom? He'd take Tom somewhere. He'd never really been anywhere himself beyond London and the suburbs just north of the city. There were all sorts of other lands and wide, wide seas. Could he write poetry without ever seeing even the seas that surrounded England? If his rich fertile imagination could be stimulated into verse by his reading, then what wonders could not travel work!

CHAPTER V

Bring Me a Tablet Whiter than a Star

THE DECISION WAS MADE for Margate, on the extreme eastern tip of England, some seventy-five miles from London, and a public coach took the two Keats brothers along the old Dover Road to Canterbury and from Canterbury the last few miles out to the coast. There the town of Margate clustered at the edge of a harbor inlet, and along the sandy beach that rimmed the harbor sat residents of the summer hotels in their rented chairs. Out on the water bobbed the bathing machines, high-wheeled covered wagons with large umbrellas attached to their sterns so that the more intrepid ladies could go bathing in the sea without being seen or stared at by men. A white stone pier stretched far out into the sea to accommodate coastwise sailing vessels and to receive the daily catch of the local fishermen.

The beach extended all along the jutting peninsula, flanked by escarpments that offered tempting miles of hiking in the daytime. For the evenings Margate had two theaters, inns, and big halls for sociables. A cheap room in one of the boardinghouses was all the Keats brothers needed, and from there, braced with a breakfast of herring, eggs, buttered toast and honey, and hot tea, they set out on a health-making day.

The brisk, tangy air, free of contamination, and long hours out-of-doors brought a hint of color back into Tom's cheeks, and he and John enjoyed their first real chance to talk at long random, willy-nilly, covering every subject, working off their fatigues and tensions by spending and squandering their endless supply of words.

"Have you told Abbey?" asked Tom.

"About what?"

"About quitting medicine."

"Oh, no. There will be time enough for that."

"He'll throw a fit and cut off your allowance."

"I'll be twenty-one in October; after that I'll tell Abbey."

"Fancy that stupid fat ox trying to understand a career in poetry!"

"Oh, he wouldn't even try—" and the brothers laughed together.

The carefree holiday combined with his sudden sense of freedom to bring forth from John Keats a further supply of words on paper, experimental words, in metered lines and rhyme schemes. A letter to George Keats in August was 142 lines of iambic pentameter, scarcely poetry, just an effusion of "prosing verse," much of it trite, here and there borrowed from Milton and Pope, filled with his new impressions: the far depth, the wavy grass, feathery clouds, the purple west, a falling star, bowers and flowers, blisses and kisses, caves and waves, mysteries of night.

He was writing! And he had all the time in the world to do it!

In September Charles Cowden Clarke received another "prosing verse" from Keats almost as long, again sprinkled with echoes of the masters who influenced him most and with whose works his mind was saturated. It was as though John Keats was cleansing his mind of his reading memories to make himself ready for real composing.

In early October John and Tom returned to town and with George took rooms at 8 Dean Street, John's earliest address in London. At last they were together—all three of them.

London to John was now the hub of the literary universe. Charles Cowden Clarke, overjoyed that Keats was to devote himself to writing, continued the task of feeding Keats's voracious reading appetite with vitalizing matter and introducing him to artists of every kind.

He held up a huge, rare, old book one day when Keats dropped in on him, and Keats's eyes lighted up at the sight of it.

"We must read it at once because it has only been loaned to me. Do you know George Chapman's translations of Homer?"

Keats shook his head. He had done some translating from the Latin himself, he recalled, and knew it to be a slow and laborious task requiring as much dedication as skill. He put out a hand to touch the book that had been published in the year of Shakespeare's death. They sat down together, and Clarke began to read aloud the story of Ulysses. He read through the conversation on the wall of Troy between Helen and the old Senators; when he reached the fifth book in which the passages telling of Ulysses' shipwreck occurred, John Keats was transfixed.

> Then forth he came, his both knees faltring; both
> His strong hands hanging downe; and all in froth
> His cheeks and nosthrils flowing. Voice and breath
> Spent all to use; and downe he sunke to Death.
> The sea had soakt his heart through; all his vaines

His toiles had rackt, t'a labouring woman's paines.
Dead weary was he.

Clarke paused and Keats stared at him for a moment. Then he cried, "*The sea had soakt his heart through!* My dear Charles, what a tremendous line! What boldness of expression! I feel as though—as though—I'd seen a new planet in the sky!"

Clarke read on and on until at last, out of sheer fatigue of voice, he closed the book in his lap, and the two littérateurs grinned at each other a little sheepishly. Their eyes were heavy, their heads ached in protest, and the windows were lighted with the first gay tones of dawn.

"I rather guess I must leave," Keats said as he rose stiffly to his feet.

Clarke was too weary to make the social pretense of delaying his departure, but he did suggest, "Come back this evening, and we will read some more."

John Keats walked home with his mind in a turmoil of creation, and ignoring the sleeping figures of his brothers went straight to his writing table.

Much have I travell'd in the realms of gold,
    And many goodly states and kingdoms seen;
    Round many western islands have I been
Which bards in fealty to Apollo hold.
Oft of one wide expanse had I been told
    That deep-brow'd Homer ruled as his demesne;
    Yet could I never tell what men could mean
Till I heard Chapman speak out loud and bold:
Then felt I like some watcher of the skies
    When a new planet swims into his ken;
Or like stout Cortez when with eagle eyes
    He star'd at the Pacific—and all his men
Look'd at each other with a wild surmise—
    Silent, upon a peak in Darien.

Art is communication; a poem is a thing to share. His sonnet, "On First Looking into Chapman's Homer," was soon completed and ready for Charles to see. What time was it? His brothers were up and about, leaving him tactfully undisturbed because they knew he was writing, and if they were up it must be seven, eight, nine. Charles would be asleep, had probably gone to bed as soon as Keats left him . . . But a poem is a thing to share . . .

He folded the piece of paper, slipped it into his pocket, and went out into the street. It teemed with people all hurrying to begin the day, and Keats hurried along among them as certain of his direction as they of theirs. He walked the whole distance back to Little Warner Street, tapped gently on the door, held a whispering conversation with the maid, slipped in and left the sonnet at Clarke's place at the breakfast table, and slipped away again. Only then, when his mission was completed, did fatigue descend upon him, and he wondered whether he would be able to walk the two miles back.

Keats soon learned that Clarke had come down to breakfast about ten that morning and had been delighted with the poem.

The distance between his own quarters and Clarke's was soon cut approximately in half, because he and his brothers moved to 76 Cheapside, a street very near St. Paul's and Pancras Lane. Keats no longer needed to be near the hospital, and his brothers were still serving their apprenticeships in Pancras Lane.

On October 31 Keats wrote Clarke a short happy note: "I will be as punctual as the Bee to the Clover. Very glad am I at the thoughts of seeing so soon this glorious Haydon and all his Creation. I pray thee let me know when you go to Ollier's. . . ."

Ollier was a young publisher who had brought out Shelley's *Alastor,* and Benjamin Robert Haydon was a painter. When Clarke escorted him to Haydon's studio in Great Marlborough Street, Keats felt a quick little *ping* of satisfaction to meet another short man. Haydon's handclasp was as strong as a giant's; his manner was bold and aggressive; he was self-willed and self-confident beyond all measure. Obviously an easy man to quarrel with, but Keats was too young to be on guard for that trait. What he saw was another artist, not quite ten years older than himself, who had revolted against apprenticeship to his bookselling and printing father and persuaded his family to let him come up to London to study painting at the Royal Academy. By the time Keats met him, Haydon had already made something of a name for himself with such paintings as "Macbeth" and "The Judgment of Solomon."

Keats stared at the huge canvas on which Haydon was then working. It covered one entire wall of the studio; it was nearly fifteen feet long and more than twelve feet high.

"But who could buy such a big canvas?" Keats blurted out.

"I shall hire a hall for it and charge admission when it is done," Haydon replied haughtily, and Keats had no idea that he meant it.

The picture was to depict Christ's entry into Jerusalem; Haydon had been working on it for more than two years and it was far from completed.

Keats and Haydon abruptly became friends, and in the months that followed their friendship deepened rapidly. On that first meeting Haydon, the recognized artist, discoursed at length to the younger hopeful, and their conversation quickly found its way to the controversy of the hour: the Elgin Marbles. Haydon brought out a stack of sketches and studies that he had been making of the Elgin Marbles and showed them to Keats.

"Lord Elgin granted me access to the marbles almost eight years ago when he first began to bring them into the country. Look at the wrist of this hand," he said to the poet-medical student, "and notice how realistically the bones are shown. Look at the perfection in the muscles of this athlete."

Lord Elgin (Thomas Bruce, Seventh Earl of Elgin) had spent his personal wealth to rescue many statues and friezes from the Parthenon in Athens. Greece at the time was under a tottering Turkish rule, and the Parthenon and its friezes and statuary were neglected, pieces of stonework pilfered by housebuilders, statues broken and abused by the soldiers stationed in Greece. Once he had the marbles in England, Lord Elgin offered them to the government, and a committee was appointed to investigate their merit. Tremendous publicity resulted from the "trial," and Haydon had been a star witness in behalf of the authenticity of the collection. His testimony had counted heavily in the decision of the government to purchase the marbles for the British Museum.

Keats, like almost everyone in England who read any published matter, had known about the Elgin Marbles incident; but until Haydon explained them to him Keats had not really realized their artistic significance. "Great spirits now on earth are sojourning," he wrote as a first line of a sonnet in tribute to Haydon, and sent it to the painter in a note, after an evening when Haydon had drawn his profile.

Keats went from introduction to introduction that autumn and winter like a young porpoise leaping through wave after wave, rising invigorated from every plunge. He met both Charles and James Ollier, the publishers, and soon after that the Reynolds family and William Hazlitt.

John Hamilton Reynolds, the same age as Keats, was a hopeful poet who had already published some works and had drawn some encouraging praise from Lord Byron. He was a member of Leigh Hunt's circle and a friend of Haydon's, although he was far gentler and less wearing a companion than the volatile Haydon.

John Keats became attached to the whole cultured and well-educated family and their associates. The father was a schoolmaster. John Reynolds's sister Jane eventually married Thomas Hood, the humorous poet, and another sister, Marianne, was being courted by a talented young Oxford man studying for holy orders, named Benjamin Bailey. Reynolds and Bailey had just done a volume of verse together when Keats made their acquaintance.

John Keats, the warm-blooded, deeply normal, rapidly maturing intellectual loved everyone he met, loved what they did, loved the courageous free thinking of many of them, their idealism, their devotion to their callings. They all seemed young! They all seemed and behaved as though they would live forever.

Yet, when he met William Hazlitt, seventeen years older than himself, moderate, objective, wise, he felt no barrier in the age difference. Hazlitt possessed both mature dignity and creative passion, and his late start as a writer kept the memory of his own artistic searching alive in his manner.

"So you know you are a poet, Keats. You are blessed indeed to discover your true vocation so young. I experimented a long time before I realized that writing is my area of art. I studied painting for a good many years."

Hazlitt wrote articles in criticism for *The Examiner* and for *The Edinburgh Review*. His opinion in art and letters counted for a great deal. He shared with Keats and many more a love and admiration of Leigh Hunt and had been one of those to call upon Hunt in prison. Keats was startled to hear Hazlitt express doubts about Haydon's long-term greatness.

Because Keats was so open-hearted and ready to admire others, he was liked and accepted in the same candid way, and anyone who met him once wanted to see him again and know him better. Keats was generous with his good fortune, spontaneously sharing it with others. All the exhilarating gossip of the world of art and artists that he was now in touch with—the increase in Tory power in England since the defeat of Napoleon at Waterloo; its counterreaction in the intellectual radical set; schisms at the Royal Academy; the behind-the-scenes story of such public debates as that on the Elgin Marbles—he passed on to anyone who needed its stimulation: to Joseph Severn lest he grow embittered, to his brothers, to his lonely young sister. And he sometimes administered verse the way a doctor would administer medicine. For Tom's seventeenth birthday he wrote:

> Small, busy flames play through the fresh-laid coals,
>   And their faint cracklings o'er our silence creep
>   Like whispers of the household gods that keep
> A gentle empire o'er fraternal souls.
> And while, for rhymes, I search around the poles,
>   Your eyes are fix'd, as in poetic sleep,
>   Upon the lore so voluble and deep,
> That aye at fall of night our care condoles.
> This is your birth-day Tom, and I rejoice
>   That thus it passes smoothly, quietly.
> Many such eves of gently whisp'ring noise
>   May we together pass, and calmly try
> What are this world's true joys,—ere the great voice,
>   From its fair face, shall bid our spirits fly.

The sonnet form, early challenge to any aspiring poet, once mastered, began to grow less satisfying, and the style of the times—long, romantic verse tales like *Childe Harold* and *Rimini*, and long philosophic poems like *The Excursion*—exerted a strong influence on Keats. "Induction" and "Calidore" and even the epistles from Margate had cast prophetic shadows ahead of them, and almost unconsciously he began to grope toward fuller expression, toward living for a long period with a single poetic effort.

An evening at Hunt's brought the longer poem into being. In the tiny parlor-study lined with books a literary evening grew so gay and ran on so late that the Hunts would not allow Keats to go home. He must remain the night, and they made up a bed for him on the sofa. Leigh and Marianne Hunt left him alone and he stretched out on his impromptu bed in the suddenly quieted room. One candle, he had told them, would be all he would need—one candle for a little while—and its wavering flame created grotesque shadows on the busts of bygone poets that stood on top of the bookcases. Keats could not sleep. He could not even close his eyes. He was overstimulated and his head rang with the "strange thunders" of the evening's conversation.

The confusions and thunders began to marshal themselves into fragments of a pattern, and Keats sat up and seized a tablet and began to sketch out his long poem, "Sleep and Poetry." His first line was:

> What is more gentle than a wind in summer?

and he was pleased with it, but he could not hold to that mature and dignified level throughout the poem. The lingering schoolboy and the emerging man wrestled together for dominance of every line, as they had been doing in everything that Keats had written so far. In "Sleep and Poetry" the boy, baffled and frustrated by the demands of craft, produced many trite lines, but the adult poet showed more strength and skill than he ever had before and set down such splendid lines as:

> sorts
> Out the dark mysteries of human souls
> To clear conceiving . . .

Keats was acutely aware of his own struggle, working on

the poem that night and later at home, for early in "Sleep and Poetry" he said:

> O Poesy! for thee I hold my pen
> That am not yet a glorious denizen
> Of thy wide heaven . . .

He understood his muse, and knew what he sought, knew

> the great end
> Of poesy, that it should be a friend
> To soothe the cares, and lift the thoughts of man.

He strove the night through to capture his muse on the tablet,

> for lovely airs
> Are fluttering round the room like doves in pairs.

and he took his incomplete results home with him next morning.

> And up I rose refresh'd, and glad, and gay,
> Resolving to begin that very day
> These lines; and howsoever they be done,
> I leave them as a father does his son.

"Glad and gay" he did indeed feel over the poem and so did brothers and friends who read it, and close upon its heels came the December 1, 1816, issue of *The Examiner*. On that Sunday morning the three Keats brothers crowded their heads together to read its pages, which contained an article entitled "Young Poets."

"The object of the present article is merely to notice three young writers, who appear to us to promise a considerable addition of strength to the new school," they read. First, the article named Percy Bysshe Shelley and called him "a very striking and original thinker." Next came John Hamilton Reynolds and the first twenty-seven lines of one of his poems quoted. "The last of these young aspirants," said the article,

was the youngest of them all. "His name is John Keats."
There followed the full text of Keats's sonnet, "On First
Looking into Chapman's Homer." It called attention to an
imperfection in the seventh line (Keats later changed it to
read, "Yet did I never breathe its pure serene"), but it called
the rest of the poem "powerful and quiet."

While the three Keats brothers shouted and talked with a
joyful clamor, Shelley was dashing up and down his street
in the city of Bath where he was living, trying to borrow a
copy of the paper from a neighbor. This morning, of all
mornings, his *Examiner* had not arrived! And when Clarke
came to his breakfast table he did what he did every Sunday
morning, snatched up *The Examiner* before tasting any food,
to find the prophecy about his protégé.

The same afternoon John Keats, Charles Cowden Clarke,
and one or two others, were milling about in Hunt's small
parlor, the glamorous, self-dramatizing Hunt loving the happy
homage, admitting that he had written the article himself.

"Too bad Shelley is at Bath," Hunt observed. "I promise
you, Keats, you shall meet him as soon as he comes up to
London."

"This is a time for music!" declared Clarke.

"Oh, yes, my dear Charles," agreed Keats.

Hunt sat down at his own pianoforte and sang a whole list
of Italian songs.

It was dark when Keats returned from Hunt's that night,
because it was winter; and it was cold. He was filled with
hope and the memory of tinkling melodies and his cheeks
tingled from the frost. His feet beat out an iambic meter as
he walked along.

> Keen, fitful gusts are whisp'ring here and there
> Among the bushes half leafless, and dry;
> The stars look very cold about the sky,
> And I have many miles on foot to fare.

> Yet feel I little of the cold bleak air,
>   Or of the dead leaves rustling drearily,
>   Or of those silver lamps that burn on high,
> Or of the distance from home's pleasant lair:
> For I am brimfull of the friendliness
>   That in a little cottage I have found;
> Of fair-hair'd Milton's eloquent distress,
>   And all his love for gentle Lycid drown'd;
> Of lovely Laura in her light green dress,
>   And faithful Petrarch gloriously crown'd.

Keats gave Clarke the sonnet soon afterward, along with the other that begins

> Give me a golden pen, and let me lean
>   On heap'd up flowers, in regions clear, and far;
>   Bring me a tablet whiter than a star . . .

And when he did so he was aware of his lessening humility toward Clarke, a lessening really of his own dependence upon Clarke. Leigh Hunt seemed to be his new literary focal point, and there was Haydon. . . . He still enjoyed showing his poems to Clarke, but he shared them now whereas a year or two earlier he had submitted them. Now he needed Clarke's understanding as a trusted friend.

"My dear Charles," he wrote on the 17th of December, 1816, "I met Reynolds at Haydon's a few mornings since. He promised to be with me this evening, and yesterday I had the same promise from Severn, and I must put you in mind that on last All Hallowmas Day you gave your word that you would spend this evening with me, so no putting off. I have done little to *Endymion* lately. I hope to finish it in one more attack."

This new poem—this new *long* poem—that he thought he would call "Endymion" would be ready for Charles. The Greek word Endymion held a particular fascination for Keats.

It hummed softly upon the lips and it scanned easily, and the legend of the beautiful young shepherd king existed for poets. Endymion had loved the moon goddess, and she exempted him from death, allowing him to remain asleep for-ever, so that she would never have to give him up. Never to die! To cheat death! Never to return to dust!

But this poem had eluded the story, or rather Endymion had eluded the poet, and John Keats decided to make a fresh start later on the Endymion story.

"Not Endymion?" Clarke asked in surprise when John Keats handed him the finished effort.

"That will be for something else," Keats explained vaguely, and leaned back to listen with eyes half closed while Charles Cowden Clarke read aloud.

> I stood tip-toe upon a little hill,
> The air was cooling, and so very still,
> That the sweet buds which with a modest pride
> Pull droopingly, in slanting curve aside,
> Their scantly leaved, and finely tapering stems,
> Had not yet lost those starry diadems
> Caught from the early sobbing of the morn.
> The clouds were pure and white as flocks new shorn,
> And fresh from the clear brook; sweetly they slept
> On the blue fields of heaven, and then there crept
> A little noiseless noise among the leaves,
> Born of the very sigh that silence heaves . . .

Clarke finished with a tone of frank humility.

"We must show Leigh Hunt," he said. "He will be de-lighted to see his prophecy coming true so soon."

> And from the pillowy silkiness that rests
> Full in the speculation of the stars.
> Ah! surely he had burst our mortal bars;
> Into some wond'rous region he had gone,
> To search for thee, divine Endymion!

CHAPTER VI

A Thing of Beauty

KEATS WAS BEGINNING to live in a slow crescendo of happy elation, accelerated by the responses of his friends and advisers to "I Stood Tip-toe." Whenever he joined an evening group he sensed the tingle of admiration and pleasure that he stimulated and the eagerness with which they drew him into their midst. His capacities were expanding, his talents flowering, and his friends—Leigh Hunt, Benjamin Haydon, John Hamilton Reynolds, Joseph Severn, the Mathews, Charles Cowden Clarke, and his brothers—had begun to urge and encourage him to collect his poems together and seek out a publisher. By the end of 1816 he had become convinced that he ought to attempt publication.

This decision made, he was more eager than ever for the advice of Leigh Hunt, and by now he came and went at Hunt's cottage almost like a member of the family, as oblivious as Hunt himself to Marianne's confused housekeeping. He would drop by for dinner, alone or with Clarke, and after dinner spend a long evening in conversation.

One December evening, talk on publication problems exhausted, Keats and Clarke were sitting before the fire with Hunt, and they fell to philosophizing about the fire in the hearth and of fireside crickets and grasshoppers.

"We are both poets, Keats!" declared Hunt, who had obviously hit upon an idea. "Let me challenge you, here and now. Let us each write a sonnet 'On the Grasshopper and Cricket,' and I say I can do it faster than you."

Keats began to search in his pockets for a tablet.

"I shall withdraw into a book until you are finished," said Clarke, and he sat down at the far end of the sofa.

There was a heavy silence in the room for a while, until John Keats laid down his tablet with a broad smile. In another moment Hunt had finished his and insisted on hearing Keats's poem first.

"The poetry of earth is never dead," Keats began.

"Such a prosperous opening!" declared Hunt.

When Keats read the lines,

> On a lone winter evening, when the frost
>   Has wrought a silence . . .

Hunt broke in again, "Ah! That's perfect! bravo, Keats!"

After Keats had finished and Hunt had read his own poem, Hunt said that John Keats had written the better one; but on the way home John Keats said to Clarke, "Charles, I do think Hunt's poem was better than mine."

He did think well enough of his own, though, to include it with others that he was selecting for publication.

The Ollier brothers, Shelley's publishers, accepted John Keats's poems, but Shelley himself protested vigorously when he heard the news.

"Oh, no, Keats!" Shelley said. "Do not publish your first blights."

Keats experienced a surge of resentment. Why should Shelley not want him to be published? Shelley had been published more than once.

The sensitive Shelley, realizing that he had offended Keats, rushed impetuously to give him every assistance in the production of the book, even going to Olliers' printers in person.

Since the publication of the article, "Young Poets," in *The Examiner*, Shelley had become a frequent caller at the Vale of Health, and so he and Keats saw one another rather often. Keats's initial meeting with Shelley had had a rather startling result. John Keats, warm-hearted, outgoing, sociable, had gone eagerly to Hunt's cottage for the prospective introduction, but had experienced a quick dislike for Shelley when he was confronted by him. There was Shelley, his effeminately beautiful face filled with candid pleasure at meeting Keats, his high-pitched, reedy voice expressing some words of greeting. Shelley was a nobleman, he had a genteel manner, and he was *tall*. Keats, middle-class, suddenly aware of his own lack of social training and height, found it difficult to be gracious, and when he saw Hunt's frank liking for Shelley he experienced a twinge of jealousy. In spite of the ease with which he usually made friends and kept them, Keats was never quite able to allow a friendship to develop between himself and Shelley.

The excitement of preparing his *Poems* for publication sustained Keats's spirits through the spring of 1817, as he conferred with Charles and James Ollier on content and format, or sat at home with his brothers correcting proofs. Interest in the forthcoming volume spread like a contagion among his friends, and on the evening when the last proof sheet came in the Keats brothers' quarters were milling with young men.

"What about a dedication, Keats?" someone asked.

"Oh, I shall dedicate it to Leigh Hunt."

"The printer must have your dedication at once, you know, if it is to be included."

Keats thought a moment.

"This calls for one more poem!" he said, and he went to a small table at the side of the room. With conversation buzzing around his head, he wrote with complete detachment and without correction, "To Leigh Hunt, Esq."

He jumped up from his chair, poem in hand, and wheeled about in triumph to the group.

"Read it, Keats!" The poet obliged:

> Glory and loveliness have passed away;
>   For if we wander out in early morn,
>   No wreathed incense do we see upborne
> Into the east, to meet the smiling day:
> No crowd of nymphs soft voic'd and young, and gay,
>   In woven baskets bringing ears of corn,
>   Roses, and pinks, and violets, to adorn
> The shrine of Flora in her early May.
> But there are left delights as high as these.
>   And I shall ever bless my destiny,
>   That in a time, when under pleasant trees
>   Pan is no longer sought, I feel a free
> A leafy luxury, seeing I could please
>   With these poor offerings, a man like thee.

And as soon as they had heard it: "Splendid! Well turned!"

"The idea came to me," said Keats, "on a delightful summer day as I stood beside the gate that leads from the battery on Hampstead Heath into a field by Caen Wood."

The last proof and the dedication sent off to the printer, John Keats was completely free to go from salon to salon, evening after evening; to Hunt's, to Haydon's; and there was another important gathering to which he had recently been invited for the first time, that in the home of Vincent Novello, the organist and composer.

On his occasional visits to the Novellos Keats always warmed at once to the large family in its modest house at 240 Oxford Street, where everyone loved and enjoyed the arts, where fine prints hung on the walls and a small organ stood in the living room. Vincent and Mary Novello extended their hospitality to almost everyone who counted in new music and letters: Hazlitt, Hunt, Haydon, Charles and Mary Lamb, Shelley, Shelley's father-in-law William Godwin, and many more. An evening with the Novellos was a feast of music, because the host always sat down at the organ and played the composers that the romantics loved: Mozart, Haydn. Keats usually had his favorite chair, close to the organ, where he sat with his head leaning against the instrument, holding one foot on his knee, his eyes closed, his imagination released by the melodies into his own cosmic world.

From Haydon's studio one early spring day he and the painter set out for the British Museum.

"I want you to see the Elgin Marbles," Haydon had said.

Thus, with an artist as raconteur and guide, Keats's growing love of things Grecian came into focus, and he experienced the full impact of "Grecian grandeur." It was almost too much, this first exposure. He had had no idea—hadn't realized —his spirit felt too weak. Since he knew no Greek, he had not had any real view of these great depths before, these "dim-conceived glories of the brain," this "magnitude." He could see now that his "Ode to Apollo," his concern with rhyming Greek words, had been juvenile. He must go back to the Museum again and again, sit with the marbles, absorb their perfection. He could! He had the time! This *was* his work.

Very shortly after that trip to the Museum, Haydon received two sonnets from John Keats: "On Seeing the Elgin Marbles" and "To Haydon."

> Haydon! forgive me that I cannot speak
> Definitively on these mighty things;
> Forgive me that I have not Eagle's wings . . .

Keats's hour of supreme intoxication arrived during the first week of March 1817, when he received copies of his book. He held one in his hand, caressed its light brown boards, turned it this way and that, studied the edges of the uncut pages, turned back the top board and looked at the title page: *Poems* by John Keats, a quotation from Spenser, a vignette portrait of Spenser, name and address of the publisher, the year of publication. It was a beautiful little volume, its pages 4¼ inches by 6¾, a convenient size to slip into a man's pocket, and it contained almost everything he had written so far: "I Stood Tip-toe," "Calidore," "Imitation of Spenser," his "Epistles," seventeen sonnets, and "Sleep and Poetry." He closed the book again and looked at the spine where a white paper label was pasted reading, "Keats's Poems, Price 6s."

Ecstasy reigned among all his friends when the volume appeared. He was their young immortal, and his poems were going to make literary history.

"He is a sound young man and will be a great one," declared the extravagant, bombastic Haydon. " 'Sleep and Poetry' is a flash of lightning that will sound men from their occupations, and keep them trembling for the crash of thunder that will follow."

Keats received sonnets of tribute from many of his admirers.

The first review—an exceptionally early one—came out on March 9, in a magazine called *The Champion*, and said: "At a time when nothing is talked of but the power and the passion of Lord Byron, and the playful and elegant fancy of Moore . . . a young man starts suddenly before us, with a genius that is likely to eclipse them all."

Drunk with joy, Keats was unable to water down the ardor

of the review with the knowledge that it was probably written by John Hamilton Reynolds. It had appeared! He had been compared to his adored Byron!

"You are going to be a sensation in the literary world!" prophesied Clarke.

The Olliers, his publishers, predicted several editions.

Several editions meant thousands of copies which in turn meant income, real income, independent of Abbey.

Abbey had reacted like a typical middle-class merchant to the idea of giving up a lucrative profession, and Keats, who was relying on the fact that he had reached his majority, had forgotten one thing: his sister Fanny was far below her majority, under Abbey's control. When Abbey learned that John Keats was throwing over his medical studies, he took one sure, shrewd way of punishing him. He refused to let John see his sister. John, the foster father, felt sick from worry about it, and he wrote to her often, filling his letters with news of himself, George and Tom, and urging her to write back.

Hoping to soften Abbey's attitude, Keats took him a copy of *Poems*. But Abbey was not through punishing John Keats. When Keats saw him again he was greeted with, "Well, John, I have read your book and it reminds me of the Quaker's horse, which was hard to catch, and good for nothing when it was caught."

Abbey! Fat, stupid, ignorant, tea peddler! There would come a day! Keats was traveling in the "realms of gold" now, realms that Abbey couldn't understand; he'd found the "endless fountain of immortal drink." What could Abbey know of immortality?

John Keats hurried away from Abbey, back to his brothers. He found Tom resting on his bed and saw a sudden expressive depth in George's eyes. Tom had a cold, his forehead was too hot, and the cough had returned to bedevil him. Compassion overwhelmed John Keats and swept everything else aside. How he loved his brothers! His affection for them was "passing the love of women."

A poet must think extravagantly, and Keats—ardent, vigorous, twenty-one—compared his love for his brothers to that of women because women were on his mind a great deal of the time. He flirted with them at parties, yearned for them, needed them, yet could not quite find his way to them. Their complication of clothing held him at bay. He sometimes studied their hair styles, trying to fathom where the scheme began and ended, knowing full well that some men plunged their fingers deep into the elaborate mystery. He had brushed and braided his mother's hair when she was ill, had pulled Fanny's; but now he was neither a young son who could reach up nor a big brother who could reach down.

He and his brothers talked often of women and their types, trying to search out and define their own longings and needs, and although John was the oldest and most worldly, since he was a published poet, he was not the first of the three brothers to fall in love. It was George, and the girl's name was Georgiana Augusta Wylie.

George and Tom had become acquainted with the Wylies soon after their arrival in town as apprentices in Abbey's business, before John came up to London, and Georgiana's parents and two brothers drew the very young and homeless orphan boys into their family circle.

Now, in 1817, Georgiana was only sixteen, and twenty-year-old George was trying to gather sufficient courage to approach her father for her hand. John supported his brother in the plan. He had liked and admired Georgiana from the first, and just the previous December he had written a saccharine sonnet to her, later including it in *Poems:*

Nymph of the downward smile and sidelong glance,
   In what diviner moments of the day
   Art thou most lovely?

"If her father refuses to allow us to become engaged, I shall die," George confided to John.

Knowing her father, John was quick to reassure George.

"Oh, you are so elated over your book that everything seems rosy to you," George protested. "You are lucky not to be in love. That would put a different color on the world for you!"

John, the published author, had to admit that the world did seem great and boundless to him. He could "peer up at the morning sun, with half-shut eyes and comfortable cheek"; hear wandering melodies wherever he cocked his ear. George's accusation was quite true, and that first review had made him feel positively taller.

But his great hope for those several editions predicted by his publishers combined with his deep sense of family responsibility, and he decided to remove both of his brothers from noisy, dirty London to Hampstead Heath. They all loved the country; so why not? The brother-in-love would feel less morbid and discouraged in an attractive surrounding; he himself could write better poetry if he were closer to nature. Tom's health was growing worse, and called for country air. Keats the doctor watched Tom's slow loss of weight and growing excitability, listened to his cough, felt his persistently too-warm cheek.

The three Keats brothers took lodgings at 1 Well Walk Hampstead, in the home of Benjamin Bentley, the local postman, and his wife. It was one of those space-saving, room-above-room houses, with the three young men occupying the top levels and the Bentleys and two noisy children below; but it was out in the country, filled with wild flowers, brooks, meadows, singing birds, stretches of wood, rolling hills, and only a short walk from Hunt's cottage. Through their windows the warm spring air blew the odors of blossoming fruit trees.

Keats was glad to be closer to Hunt, because Clarke, from whom he had been drifting slowly for some time, had finally gone out of his immediate life altogether. He had moved out to Ramsgate, not far from Margate, on the eastern tip of England. Their relationship was reduced to correspondence and an occasional meeting.

In the pleasanter atmosphere of Well Walk, Keats watched young Tom improve in both spirit and health, and waited for more reviews of *Poems*. On the first of April another favorable review came out in *The Monthly Magazine;* only a paragraph long, to be sure, and not in a major magazine, but it referred to "the sweetness and beauty of the compositions" and called them "a revelry of the imagination and tenderness of feeling."

Surely this must be a trend! His intoxication renewed, Keats strode up to London and hurried to show the review to Haydon. He found the roughhewn artist where he knew he would find him, in his studio at 22 Lisson Grove North, just west of Regent's Park, the larger quarters into which he had recently moved.

"Come in, Keats!"

Keats obeyed and flushed with pleasure to see the mounted life-mask that Haydon had recently made of him. Life-masks were fashionable then and were made by molding wet clay or soft wax to the face of the subject, with straws in his nostrils to permit his breathing until the material set. Then the mold was removed and filled with plaster, thus producing a perfect replica of his features. Near Keats's mask stood one of William Wordsworth.

The masks were more than a fad to Haydon. He was

planning to use the faces of Keats and Wordsworth in the
crowd of spectators in his huge canvas, "Christ's Entry into
Jerusalem." Hazlitt had just finished sitting for him.

Keats handed Haydon the review and then took a step
well back so that he could study and admire the progress
of the painting. Hazlitt's head seemed extremely well done
to him. Suddenly Keats's sensitive face grew brighter as he
recognized another head in the painting, that of Voltaire,
advocate of free thought, high priest of many in Keats's set.
Keats at once made himself taller, laid his hand upon his heart,
and pronounced, "There is the being I will bow to!"

"Oh, no, Keats! That is not why I included his face in the
crowd. He merely represents a type; his *features* interested
me, that is all. Come here and sit down."

Keats complied amiably because he had been more or less
ragging Haydon, knowing Haydon to be a deeply religious
man. Haydon began to talk long and earnestly, pleading with
him to listen less to Leigh Hunt, to hold himself more aloof
from Hunt's coterie. They were too influenced by the French
Revolution and Napoleon and Italy. Look at *Rimini!* And
Byron was living in Italy.

"Be cautious of that group, Keats! They will corrupt you.
Do not spend so much time with them. Develop yourself in-
dependently."

John Keats loved and needed intellectual company, and
Benjamin Haydon understood that, and so he urged Keats to
come oftener to his own studio, promised to introduce him
to Wordsworth some day.

"If I am working, you can read quietly here. You won't
disturb me."

Slowly a competition was developing between Haydon and
Hunt for domination of Keats, and while Hunt was the liberal
and free thinker, it was Haydon who made the less selfish

suggestion, when he learned what it was that Keats wanted to write next.

"Get away from everyone," said Haydon. "Take a few weeks away somewhere *alone.* Separate yourself from all of these influences—and create *your* poem."

This poem was to be Keats's second attempt to seek out the legend of Endymion and develop it, the legend of the shepherd king who fell in love with the moon goddess and was granted the power to forestall death.

"This poem—*Endymion*—is to be long," he hurried to tell Haydon. "Much longer than anything I have ever written before."

Haydon nodded with complete understanding, because he sought bigger and bigger canvases to satisfy himself, and so it was perfectly clear to him why John Keats must write a *longer* poem, much longer than anything he had done before. He would have liked Keats simply to disappear from town and write, but the garrulous Keats could not do it that way. He told his brothers immediately.

"Go by yourself into the country," they agreed.

He consulted many of his host of friends and the consensus seemed to be that the isolation and mild climate of the Isle of Wight would be ideal for him. Some mentioned the village of Carisbrooke, others the shore resort of Shanklin on Wight.

When Percy Bysshe Shelley heard that Keats needed a retreat in which to write, he invited him to the house he and Mary had recently leased at Marlow, on the Thames, some thirty miles west of London. John Keats knew that in the charming English village of Marlow he would have lovely meadows and wooded hills rolling up away from the river, and boating on the river with Shelley. Shelley, who was then writing his *Revolt of Islam,* declared Marlow a beautiful place to work.

But Keats declined Shelley's invitation that he might have

his "own unfettered scope," and set off for Southhampton on the fourteenth of April, planning to go on from there to the Isle of Wight.

Exhilarated by the idea of traveling, Keats rode on top of the coach, enjoying the "dusty hedges," ponds, blooming furze, wooded stretches, "park palings," and grazing cows, rocking his body slightly to the motion of the vehicle and its trotting horses, forgetting the name of each town he passed through as soon as he had heard it. But as "the lamplight crept along," the air grew damp and chill, his spirits began to sink, and he climbed down at one of the stops to ride inside during the night. In the unheated, jouncing interior, loneliness settled upon him. He wanted to talk to someone and there was no one. If only George or Tom had come with him, or perhaps Reynolds, Mathew, Haydon, or Severn. He could not write if he was going to feel so desolate away from them all.

The bright morning gave his spirits a turn upward, and the bustling old port of Southhampton, its "shores on each side stretching to the Isle of Wight," restored them still further. He went to an inn for breakfast, and as soon as the hot tea had taken effect set out to inquire about the boat out to Wight. It would not go until three. Well, then, he would while away his morning exploring Southhampton, and by the time he stopped for his midday meal—a chop—he was ready to write a chronicle home to his brothers about his journey so far.

That afternoon a sailing vessel carried him across the four miles of water to the deep harbor of Cowes, and he rode inland another four-and-a-half miles to Newport. There he had a choice to make: Shanklin on the eastern coast of the island or Carisbrooke about a mile away. There was really no hurry. Why not look at both? He set out first for Shanklin.

"Shanklin is a most beautiful place," he wrote home to

Reynolds, "sloping wood and meadow ground reaches around the Chine [rock formations created by the sea], which is a cleft between the cliffs of the depth of nearly 300 feet at least." There was a long stretch of beach, and there were trees and primroses, green hedges and fishermen's huts. But Shanklin, he found, was also quite expensive, and so he returned inland to the village of Carisbrooke.

Carisbrooke did not have a view of the sea, but it had beauty. In fact, the whole Isle of Wight was delightfully picturesque, full of rolling green hills, rich pastoral valleys, and the air was both mild and refreshing. He took rooms with a Mrs. Cooke, and from his window he could see Carisbrooke Castle to the south, perched on its own hill, its imposing round turrets half covered with ivy. Yes, this was the place to work on that long poem.

From his luggage he took his volumes of Shakespeare and Spenser that he had brought along for comfort, his writing paper—coarse-surfaced, handmade rag, eight-inches-by-ten— his pens and ink, and what few items of clothing there had been room for. And so to *Endymion*. But the memory of the sea washing up on the coast at Shanklin was too vivid, and before he could proceed it had to be exorcised by the writing of a sonnet:

> It keeps eternal whisperings around
>   Desolate shores, and with its mighty swell
>   Gluts twice ten thousand caverns, till the spell
> Of Hecate leaves them their old shadowy sound . . .

His spirits began to flag again, his energy to fall away, and he took a brisk walk through the hills to restore himself. Returning to his rooms, he sat down at his writing table once more. This time it would go.

Spread out before him was a sheet of paper with a title at

the top: *"Endymion,* Book I." In his hand he held an old, old note containing a single line:

> A thing of beauty is a joy forever.

He began to write slowly under his title:

> A thing of beauty is a joy forever:
> Its loveliness increases; it will never
> Pass into nothingness . . .

all leading into the theme of death, mysterious and inevitable death, changer of patterns, destroyer of beauty, yet endowed by man's imagination with strange beauties of its own:

> the grandeur of the dooms
> We have imagined for the mighty dead;
> All lovely tales that we have heard or read:
> An endless fountain of immortal drink,
> Pouring unto us from the heaven's brink.
> . . . .
> so I will begin
> Now while I cannot hear the city's din . . .

But the beginning was slow, difficult, and the beautiful young shepherd king did not move out upon the wooded mountain-side of Latmos.

With each additional day that he spent in Carisbrooke, Keats grew more lonely and less able to write. Inhibited and frustrated, he lay down at night to stare wide-eyed at the ceiling, as worry phantoms began to gather around him, worry about Fanny, George, the ailing Tom.

"Isle of Wight will not do!" he decided and began to pack his bag.

He took a boat back to the mainland, dispatched a quick note to Tom telling him to meet him at Margate, and set out along the coast.

Margate offered the balm of familiar surroundings, so famil-

iar that they could be ignored, while he conjured up the
mountains of Greece; and Tom's prompt arrival vanquished
his loneliness and worry. To free his mind further, he began
receiving long letters from his friends.

Keats plunged into a phase of feverish productivity, working as many as eight hours a day lest his inspiration escape him.
Herds began to graze on Latmos, and

> Man's voice was on the mountains; and the mass
> Of nature's lives and wonders puls'd tenfold . . .

A troop of children, young damsels, a venerable priest, all
began to appear before a marble altar to pay their respects
to Pan. At last in the chariot and garments of a chieftain, the
beautiful Endymion entered the scene, "without a forest
peer."

But after a week of overexpending his creative energies,
another inhibiting stoppage occurred with its sleeplessness and
tensions. Margate was suddenly a barren place with absolutely
no trees. He must move on, go somewhere else, he must seek
another change of scene. And so he and Tom returned inland
to the old cathedral city of Canterbury. There in inexpensive
and obscure quarters Keats's muse returned to him, and soon
young Endymion lay out upon the mountainside at night
watching the Milky Way, until "the loveliest moon" emerged
from behind the clouds, so "passionately bright" that she
dazzled his soul. It was a dream, Endymion thought, as the
moon changed into the "naked comeliness" of the moon goddess. She approached Endymion, and the young shepherd
was "straightway into frightful eddies swoop'd."

Keats wrote with increasing heat and crystal-clear poesy.

> madly did I kiss
> The wooing arms which held me, and did give
> My eyes at once to death: but 'twas to live,
> To take in draughts of life from the gold fount

Of kind and passionate looks; to count, and count
The moments, by some greedy help that seem'd
A second self, that each might be redeem'd
And plunder'd of its load of blessedness.
Ah, desperate mortal! I ev'n dar'd to press
Her very cheek against my crowned lip,
And, at that moment, felt my body dip
Into a warmer air: a moment more
Our feet were soft in flowers.

Keats worked at Canterbury until he reached a natural
stopping point in his poem, the conclusion of Book I.

This said, he rose, faint-smiling like a star
Through autumn mists, and took Peona's hand:
They stept into the boat, and launch'd from land.

He decided to replenish himself with a holiday before starting
Book II, and he sent Tom back to George in Hampstead and
wandered down the Channel coast.

CHAPTER VII

What the Imagination Seizes

"JOHN WILL BE IN TOWN again soon . . . He sojourns at Bo-Peep near Hastings," George Keats wrote to Joseph Severn.

John Keats had found his way to Hastings, a fashionable seaside community that stood against the sloping north side of a gentle inlet. Before it stretched a flat beach and behind it rose lofty rock-cliffs topped by the fragments of an ancient castle. But again the place of his first choice proved too costly and he took accommodations in the village of Bo-Peep that lay next to Hastings on its west. Here he made no attempt to write. He went for long walks on the cliffs, climbed among the heavy rocks that littered the coast, or watched the clumsy bathing machines in the undulating water.

In the evening he wandered along the water's edge and watched his moon goddess as she "brooded o'er the water" as "glowworms began to trim their starry lamps . . . Chilly and numb his bosom grew."

As he stood watching the moon one night, a cloud floated

in front of it, and the cloud became shaped like a woman's head, a scarf blowing in the wind like a "fluttering pavilion." Was he borrowing Endymion's madness? Sweet madness! He'd make a poem of it! He ran toward the apparition, and he saw at once that it was a woman of flesh and blood who had merely walked between him and the moon. There was enough light to reveal her smile when he drew close, and before he could feel embarrassed by his own bold, impulsive approach, she spoke reassuringly:

"I've seen you so often walking along the cliffs and the shore in the last few days," she said.

"Then may we not walk together?"

She consented graciously and their conversation at first was halting and at random. To Keats his new companion seemed rather indifferently educated, although she did admire Napoleon, liked reading and music. She clearly preferred to have him do the talking and proved an avid listener, discovering quickly his favorite subject: poetry.

"I find that I cannot exist without poetry," he told her. "Half the day will not do. I began with a little, but habit has made me a Leviathan. I must go back to writing it soon, because I'm beginning to feel all of a tremble from not having written anything of late."

"Who are you?" she asked.

"John Keats," he told her. "And you?"

"Isabella Jones. Please use my first name."

Suddenly she noticed that the dampness of the sand was penetrating her shoes, and so they retraced their steps toward the lights of Hastings.

"I have an attractive sitting room," said Isabella. "Do come in and take a glass of claret with me."

Once indoors she unwound the scarf that protected her hat and hair, and under the light she did seem rather older than he, but not much. She had a blooming attractiveness, and her cheeks were pink from the wind.

They sat together sipping wine and talking. Isabella prompted him with an occasional question. Were the reviews of his book good? What of his brothers? What was his sister's name? Did they have many good times together?

As the wine began to take effect Keats's mood grew gayer and gayer, and he talked with greater abandon. There was the time that he and his two brothers went to a bear baiting!

"Have you ever seen a bear baiting?" he asked tactlessly.

"Oh, no! Ladies don't!" she reminded him with a minxish smile.

Then nothing would do but he must describe the whole thing, and when words failed he leaped up to do an imitation of the bear in the middle of the room. The great beast, he explained, rose on his hind legs—like this!—and turned to right and left as the dogs barked and snapped at him; and John Keats lumbered and swayed across the room like an angry, confused bear, his hands hanging limp in front of him like paws, now and then taking a swipe at an imaginary mongrel.

"Bravo, bravo!" called Isabella, laughing merrily. "You are a born actor!"

"Do you like the theater?" he asked, rushing impulsively back to her side. "Do you like the theater? I go often in London, and so do my friends."

"I am sometimes in London," she answered vaguely.

He realized that he had taken tight hold of both her hands, and he lifted them to his lips. *His* moon goddess wasn't cold and ethereal like Endymion's. His was made of warm flesh, and all at once he discovered that her arms and her lips were generous and willing and encouraging.

> And, at that moment, felt my body dip
> Into a warmer air: a moment more
> Our feet were soft in flowers.

He walked back to his own quarters in Bo-Peep that night under a sky full of stars, his head filled with spinning, dancing images, and only when he reached his own room did he realize that the night air had chilled him through. He lay in the dark for quite a while shivering before he fell asleep; but in the morning he awoke completely refreshed, and as soon as he had breakfasted wandered out upon the cliffs behind Hastings. He'd wait until it was properly late enough . . .

But when he called at the inn he was told that Mrs. Jones had left, that she had taken the morning stage to London.

> And does it indeed end
> Abrupt in middle air?

John Keats walked out of doors.

> He did not rave, he did not stare aghast,
> For all those visions were o'ergone, and past,
> And he in loneliness . . .

He wandered out onto the beach.

> Wherefore delay,
> Young traveller, in such a mournful place?

No reason at all to delay. He had merely come down here for a brief rest between Books I and II of *Endymion!* He returned to Bo-Peep for his things and boarded a stage to London. Sitting in the corner of the seat of the jouncing, swaying vehicle, his whirling fancies began to spin out the first lines of Book II:

> O sovereign power of love! O grief! O balm!
> All records, saving thine, come cool, and calm . . .

At Well Walk he found George ecstatically happy over his engagement to Georgiana Wylie and Tom alarmingly thinner. He sat down immediately and told them of his flirtation with the lady of Hastings, and it surprised him that neither of his brothers was particularly pleased about it.

"Forget her," said George.

Such advice was more easily given than followed. There was the image of her scarf fluttering in front of the moon, the memory of her warmth and experience.

What did blur Isabella's memory at least temporarily was the appearance of three thoughtful articles on his *Poems* in *The Examiner* for June 1, July 6 and 13. In them Leigh Hunt gave John Keats his rightful place among the poets of what Hunt termed "a very great change" that poetry was undergoing, set into motion by the Lake Poets. With genuine objectivity Hunt admitted that Keats's poetry still suffered from the faults of inexperience: "a passion for beauties, and a young impatience to vindicate them"; but he wanted the public to watch John Keats very carefully for the next ten years, because Keats had a gift for harmony, "a fine ear, a fancy and imagination at will, and an intense feeling of external beauty in its most natural and least expressible simplicity."

If Hunt felt this way about him, and if his opinion could circulate all over England, the poetry-reading public should need no further direction or advice than that. Yet, where were the sales? Most of the first edition lay on Olliers' shelves gathering dust.

"The book might have emerged in Timbuktu with stronger chance of fame and favor," remarked one of Keats's friends.

The explanation, or *an* explanation, was not hard to arrive at. John Keats had dedicated his book to Leigh Hunt the anti-Tory; Keats was a member of the liberal set himself in a time when conservatism and orthodoxy were supreme. The powerful Tory periodicals damned his book by ignoring it.

George Keats found this explanation unsatisfactory, and he penned an angry letter to the Olliers laying the blame at their door. The Olliers had their answer ready: "By far the greater number of persons who have purchased it from us have found fault with it in such plain terms, that we have in many cases offered to take it back rather than be annoyed with the ridicule . . ."

John Keats himself was quick to tell the Olliers that he felt they were not promoting his book properly, if at all, and they need not expect him to bring them his next one. It would go to Taylor and Hessey of 93 Fleet Street.

John Taylor, himself a young visionary, had already met Keats at one of the multitude of literary gatherings he frequented and declared that in his opinion Keats could not fail to become a great poet. Richard Woodhouse, an attorney connected with the firm of Taylor and Hessey, shared Taylor's enthusiasm.

Keats's confidence in Hunt, damaged somewhat by Haydon's recent advice, had been renewed by the articles in *The Examiner,* and so he showed Hunt Part I of *Endymion.* He was considerably startled and taken aback by Hunt's lack of enthusiasm for *Endymion,* and for the first time thought he detected a streak of vanity in some of his objections. Perhaps Haydon was right about Hunt after all. Perhaps he ought to be more cautious of the influence of that group. He must forget everyone and settle down to work on his next book.

But settling down to work was not at all easy, now that he was bedeviled by two disappointments. His hope of book sales and his moon goddess had both vanished into the firmament.

He sought out his friends, his ever-growing multitude of friends, going often to the theater and talking over the play afterward until late into the night. The lighthearted Reynolds was a comfort, and his friendship with Joseph Severn was becoming a real resource. Mathew's devotion was unshakable; he had recently written in *The European Magazine* a review of *Poems,* prophesying "boldly of the future eminence of our young poet" and classing Keats extravagantly with Byron and Moore. And there was a young man who had recently become a permanent admirer of Keats, James Rice, friend of both the Reynoldses and of Benjamin Bailey, the Oxford divinity student. Rice was no poet, nor did he hope to be one; he was a successful attorney who enjoyed stimulating company.

But this whirl of life among the artistic set in London raised another problem: money. True, none of them had much, except possibly Shelley, and so their attitude deemphasized the importance of wealth, but with the three Keats brothers the question was becoming one of existence. John had received his quarter share of the thousand pounds left to them by his grandfather John Jennings, and in less than a year George would come of age and receive his quarter, but all three brothers were living on the money, and George —in love—felt a real need of stylish clothing. Before the three young men had moved to Well Walk, George had left Abbey's employ and Tom was not well enough to work. Thus all of them had forfeited Abbey's compassion. They could not expect him to understand why neither John nor George was earning a shilling.

John was capable of but one choice—to write another book —and he did gradually settle down to the second part of *Endymion*, and Taylor and Hessey advanced him twenty pounds on it.

> Brain-sick shepherd-prince,
> What promise hast thou faithful guarded since
> The day of sacrifice? Or, have new sorrows
> Come with the constant dawn upon thy morrows?
> Alas! 'tis his old grief. For many days,
> He has been wandering in uncertain ways . . .

"Smothering fancies" intruded, the memory of a scarf fluttering in front of the moon, visions of English readers hurrying into English bookshops to ask for copies of "I stood tip-toe upon a little hill," and "What is more gentle than a wind in summer?"

John Keats held himself doggedly to his writing table for as long as he could each day, and, something of a stint accomplished, went earnestly out to join his friends. Oh, he needed his friends, and he needed that stimulant peculiarly essential to him: new friendships. The initial growth period of a new friendship nourished his mind in an exceptional way. Personalities were a language to him, and he absorbed their substance as he absorbed substance from the printed page. Charles Cowden Clarke, Astley Cooper, Leigh Hunt, William Hazlitt, Benjamin Robert Haydon, John Hamilton Reynolds, Benjamin Bailey, James Rice, Joseph Severn, George Felton Mathew, were parts of a continuous progression of human experiences, and the progression was to go on. The importance of Clarke to Keats's growth had by now been concluded; Hunt was no longer a growing boy's idol but an adult man's friend; his relationship with Haydon rose and fell with Haydon's volatile changes of disposition; he was becoming more intimate with Reynolds; and the richest phase of his friendship with Severn was still in the future. New friendships were a warm light toward which he constantly turned his face.

He had lived in Well Walk only a few months when the Dilkes became part of his life, and with them the balding, stoutish, happy bachelor, Charles Armitage Brown. The Dilkes and Brown had built a house together in what is now Keats Grove, Hampstead, and called it Wentworth Place. The double house, made of brick covered with white stucco, was less than half a mile southeast of Well Walk, about the same distance that Hunt's cottage in the Vale of Health was to the northwest, an easy, pleasant walk of an afternoon.

Charles Wentworth Dilke, six years older than Keats, his

wife Maria and their small son lived in the larger half of the house, and Brown in the smaller half, and Keats found his way there almost as often as he did to Vale of Health. Maria was a proper housewife, a good manager, a charming hostess, loving, motherly, unselfish, and John Keats turned unconsciously to the mother image that she suggested, prattling to her of his family, the loss of his mother, his sister, his brother Tom's poor health.

"Bring your brothers to see me," she encouraged him. "Bring them here often."

Dilke worked in the Navy Pay Office as a clerk, and he dabbled in literature, doing some writing of his own, occasionally editing volumes of collected works. Keats often met the same approximate group there that he did at Hunt's.

His more intimate friendship was with the self-indulgent Brown on the other side of the wall that divided the two semi-detached houses. Brown was the London agent for a merchant brother in India, a job that took very little effort and provided for his personal needs. And so he simply lived for each day as it came along and had a keen eye for the maid-of-all-work who occupied the basement: a curious and yet very constructive friendship for John Keats. The jocular Brown could evaluate his "heartbreak" as chagrin and his "sovereign power of love" as a passing fancy, without giving offense.

"I don't think you're in love with your lady of Hastings, Keats."

Keats wasn't convinced.

"Don't *wish* yourself into being in love, Keats; that could send you to morbid depths. The cure for one is another, my dear fellow. Look about you!"

But what Keats saw when he looked about him was his brother George's happiness at his impending marriage to Georgiana Wylie, and his mind was filled constantly with

Endymion, victim of an exotic metaphysical love, soon to be torn by a dual love for his other-world moon goddess and for his human Indian maiden. Keats and Endymion, the poet and the lover, roamed distraught, each seeking his fulfillment, in love, perfection, beauty, truth; each suffering the inhibitions of his own unsatisfied search.

By the time he reached the end of Book II, John Keats experienced another sterile lapse, when language and ideas would not come together.

> The visions of the earth were gone and fled—
> He saw the giant sea above his head.

As usual, he shared the problem with everyone, the way he usually shared so much about himself, and the Reynolds family came forward with a solution. Their young friend, Benjamin Bailey, suitor of Marianne Reynolds, was at Magdalen College, Oxford, studying for holy orders. Surely Keats must remember him. Keats not only remembered him, he remembered Bailey with very kindly feelings, had met him at the Reynoldses a few months before, at Bailey's urgent request. The Reynoldses had sent Bailey a copy of Keats's *Poems* early in the spring of 1817, and Bailey at once declared, "Keats is indeed a poet of rare and original genius. He has an exquisite mind!"

"Let us write to him for you, Keats. Perhaps you can stay with him at Oxford for a while. It may prove a good place to work."

An exchange of notes with Bailey resulted in Keats's setting off for Oxford to stay in Bailey's quarters at Magdalen, and there he had the solitude and silence of the deserted dormitory while Bailey and the other students were at lectures, the beauty of the ancient, historic scholars' town to rest his eyes on no matter what window he looked out of, Bailey's library to read, and the company of keen intellects in the late afternoon and still-light autumn evenings.

The river Cherwell, brown, peaceable, curved through wooded lands, past the college with its spired, square bell tower, under the many-arched Magdalen Bridge, until it found its way into the Thames. On its waters Keats and Bailey could paddle their way along, or drift with the current, chatting, or waiting for the sounds of birds, and on its waters Keats's moon goddess studied her silvery image through the branches of the overhanging trees.

In such a verdant, dreamlike atmosphere line after line of Book III was produced.

> O Love! how potent hast thou been to teach
> Strange journeyings! Wherever beauty dwells,
> In gulf or aerie, mountains or deep dells,
> In light, in gloom, in star or blazing sun,
> Thou pointest out the way, and straight 'tis won.

In anguish the confused, enslaved Endymion went "along his fated way," and he tasted deeply of the mysteries of life,

> . . . mouldering scrolls,
> Writ in the tongue of heaven . . .

There was no escape from destiny for Endymion; something in the moon had moved his heart so potently that he was helpless.

> 'Who could resist? Who in this universe?
> She did so breathe ambrosia; so immerse
> My fine existence in a golden clime.
> She took me like a child of suckling time,
> And cradled me in roses. Thus condemn'd,
> The current of my former life was stemm'd . . .'

Endymion went on in his search, "stumbled down a precipitous path . . . came to a dark valley" . . . met the wicked Circe . . . "fled three days" through the wild forest . . . laid

his hand upon "a dead thing's face" and found it to be Scylla
. . . "left poor Scylla in a niche and fled" . . . passed through
these evil depths until he evolved upon a more attractive
group.

> Cupid, empire-sure,
> Flutter'd and laugh'd, and oft-times through the throng
> Made a delighted way. Then dance, and song,
> And garlanding grew wild; and pleasure reign'd,

until Apollo, most beautiful and splendid of all the Greek
gods, appeared in his chariot.

The poem in Book III grew more and more mystical:

> 'Breathe softly, flutes;
> Be tender of your strings, ye soothing lutes;
> Nor be the trumpet heard! O vain, O vain;
> Not flowers budding in an April rain,
> Nor breath of sleeping dove, nor river's flow—'

Endymion had strayed so far from mortality that he could
not bear it. But if he could not find his sweet mistress, what
then? He sank into a swoon and the kindly Nereids swarmed
around him, "interwove their cradling arms and purposed to
convey" him "towards a crystal bower," when he heard the
voice of his beloved, "Awake! Awake!"

> The youth at once arose: a placid lake
> Came quiet to his eyes; and forest green,
> Cooler than all the wonder he had seen,
> Lull'd with its simple song his fluttering breast.
> How happy once again in grassy nest!

In Oxford the language flowed and flourished and multiplied under Keats's pen, and there during the month of
September he produced along with *Endymion* some of the
earlier of the wealth of letters that have endeared him to the
world as much as his poetry. To Jane and Marianne Reyn-

olds: "Here am I among colleges, halls, stalls, plenty of trees, thank God—plenty of water, thank heaven—plenty of books, thank the muses—plenty of snuff, thank Sir Walter Raleigh." To John Reynolds: some thoughts on Wordsworth. To his sister Fanny: some guidance on her reading, hoping he may adapt his scribblings to her pleasure, a paragraph about "a young handsome shepherd who fed his flocks on a mountain's side called Latmos. He was a very contemplative sort of a person and lived solitary among the trees and plains." He gave her the news of himself: "This Oxford, I have no doubt, is the finest city in the world; it is full of old Gothic buildings, spires, towers, quadrangles, cloisters, groves, and is surrounded with more clear streams than ever I saw together. I take a walk by the side of one of them every evening." Tom and George had taken a short trip to Paris, he told her.

He let Haydon know that he was getting on splendidly with his long poem.

John Keats returned to Hampstead at the end of September with the completed Book III. His brothers were home from the Continent by then, and they wanted to know at once what progress he had made.

"Is the book finished?"

Oh, no! it wasn't finished; there was still another whole section to write. "It will be a test, a trial of my powers of imagination and chiefly of my invention which is a rare thing indeed."

He did not want to talk about *Endymion* just then; he wanted to talk about Tom. Tom's appearance shocked and disturbed him, and to his doctor's eye the signs of possible consumption were clear. Tom must do no more traveling; he must spend long hours in bed each day. John talked passionately to his younger brother, pleaded with him to take better care of himself, persistently helped him undress and slip into bed, stayed by his side until the boy dozed off.

"I'll sit with him," George promised.

With one last glance at Tom's hot cheeks John wandered out of doors. He could lose them both, he realized in that instant. George was going to be married in May and was talking of going to America with his bride. Plunging down Endymion's "precipitous path" into his "dark valley" of despair, John stood hesitant for a moment at the edge of the road, wondering which way to turn, to Hunt's or to the Dilkes and Brown. In the house behind him the Bentley children were kicking up a devilish row, and he hoped they would not waken Tom. At last he turned his back on Hunt's erratic household with its own complement of children and walked toward Wentworth Place. There he moved into the warm, harmonious family circle of the Dilkes and saw their alarm at his downcast spirits.

Had he worked too hard at Oxford? Had he overexpended himself? Perhaps his depression was merely intellectual fatigue. Yes, yes, he agreed, sinking into a chair. That must be partly it, but more than that he was worried about Tom.

"I'll come over and see Tom some afternoon soon," Mrs. Dilke promised, and in spite of his depression Keats had to smile gratefully at her.

As the weather grew colder and the days shorter, every incident seemed to feed Keats's despondency. He dropped in at Haydon's studio one day to find both Hunt and Shelley there. Hunt was pacing back and forth in front of the big canvas of "Christ's Entry," "most unmercifully criticizing every head" in it. Haydon's dislike of Hunt had never shown more clearly. Another time Keats learned that Hunt had been boasting to Reynolds that he had done a severe editing job on *Endymion*, had saved it from going to 7,000 lines. If Hunt would say that to Reynolds, what would he not say to others?

"Everyone seems at loggerheads," Keats wrote to Bailey at Oxford with frank discouragement. "I am quite disgusted with literary men and will never know another except Wordsworth—no, not even Byron. . . . There's Horace Smith tired of Hunt."

But Brown—good-natured, optimistic Charles Armitage Brown—there was a refreshing fellow! Brown's spirits never sank below the norm, and his physical energies never ran out. Oh, true, he did some writing, had once written the libretto for a successful comic opera; but there was no disturbance in his soul that needed to search out great Truths or make mystical excursions among the pagan gods. Brown was a genuine tonic, and Keats spent a day with him every so often after his return from Oxford. Gradually, under the gentle prodding and poking of Brown's joviality, Keats's despondency began to dissolve.

He was sitting in Brown's little parlor in Wentworth Place one afternoon when Reynolds dropped in and added his own sunny disposition. Keats wanted to know all that had happened in Reynolds's life during the past several weeks. What had he been writing? Was there to be another volume of verse from him? Keats poured out so much of himself to others that he expected others to do the same, and Reynolds often did, but this day he was rather reticent about himself. At last Reynolds admitted:

"I am considering reading for the law. James Rice thinks I'll do well at it."

"Sensible fellow," declared Brown.

But John Keats was shocked. How could a poet give up his poetry? Had Reynolds forgotten the marvelous prediction Hunt had made of him and Shelley and himself in *The Examiner?* Reynolds had not forgotten; he was simply about to make a decision—to settle down to earning a living at law—because he knew better than Hunt what lay within himself.

"I merely had a flair for poetry," Reynolds began to explain, but the expression of incredulity on Keats's face stopped him, and he asked, "What of your *Endymion?*"

Keats described how far he had progressed in the story and confessed his high hopes for it.

"I shall complete it in another few weeks," Keats promised Brown and Reynolds.

But he was unable to keep that promise, because another incident intervened: his first illness.

Intensive, creative effort and family worries had reduced his resistance, and damp, rainy, chill weather of late autumn had done the rest. It was really a minor upset that he could medicate himself, but it kept him indoors for two weeks and shook his confidence in his own endurance. Illness he had unconsciously identified in his mind with others, casting himself in the role of nurse-doctor. He must not grow ill; he must be more careful; Tom needed him; so did Fanny.

"I shall never be again secure in robustness," he wrote to Bailey.

His recovery was sharply implemented by a favorable review of *Poems* in the October issue of Constable's *Edinburgh Magazine*, an independent and respected periodical. The review was nearly four pages long, quoted his verses copiously; it was careful, objective in its evaluations, and in no way blind to Keats's youth and the faults in his writing. It even warned him to be wary of the influences of the school to which he was attached, but it was warm-hearted and encouraging, just what he needed to throw off that lingering feeling of weakness and return to his writing table.

By the last day of October Keats was able to send Jane Reynolds his roundelay, "O Sorrow!" which makes up a portion of Book IV of *Endymion*.

Just as sharply, another October article—and issues were delivered indifferently late rather than early in the nineteenth century—burst upon the literary scene. It was entitled "On the Cockney School of Poetry" and appeared in the powerful literary publication in Edinburgh, *Blackwood's Magazine*, of Tory views. It was essentially an assault upon Leigh Hunt, but it promised a whole series of articles flaying and flailing some of the most outstanding romantics. It spoke of the "extreme moral depravity of the Cockney School" and said that Hunt talked "indelicately like a tea-sipping milliner girl" and called him fond of indecency. The article itself went on to use cruder language than the writers it was attacking in its effort to defame Hunt's reputation.

Hunt raged about the article, wrote to the magazine demanding the identity of the author, and his devotees angrily renamed the periodical "Blackguard's Magazine." In November the second in the series appeared and its language was more scurrilous than the previous one. Obviously the whole Hunt circle was going to have its turn at being maligned, and John Keats felt sickish as he read the articles and discussed them with Hunt and others. Where was a poet's freedom in a world that penalized his literary reputation for his political views? Hunt told Keats he could not afford to bring legal action for the libel against his personal character.

"I never read anything so virulent," Keats wrote to Bailey, "accusing him of the greatest crimes, depreciating his wife, his poetry, his habits, his company, his conversation . . ."

Edinburgh and London vied with one another in those days for dominance of the literary scene, particularly the periodicals, and so the Tory *Quarterly Review* in London soon gleefully entered the field, adding its own assaults to what *Blackwood's* had dubbed the "Cockney School."

A premonition crept into Keats's thinking for Endymion's fate in the Tory press. Endymion was becoming almost like a real person to be worried about, along with Tom and the isolated Fanny, rather than an earth-free, time-free allegory.

Perhaps Endymion's sorrow had become too mortal. In the first hundred lines of Book IV he had met and fallen in love with a mortal maiden, and yet he still felt inevitably bound to his moon goddess.

> Upon a bough
> He leant, wretched. He surely cannot now
> Thirst for another love: O impious,
> That he can even dream upon it thus!—

The maiden, realizing she must lose him, sang her roundelay, "O Sorrow!" and the song so moved Endymion that he changed his mind about leaving the Indian maiden.

> I've no choice;
> I must be thy sad servant evermore.

Sad servant on a mortal level! His creator a sad servant to mortal problems, finding it impossible to soar with Endymion while his brother coughed, while he listened to George talking of his fascination for America, while angry thoughts fumed up in him whenever he glanced at the copy of "Blackguard's Magazine." There were only some five hundred more lines of *Endymion* to write and his story would be finished.

"Tom has improved somewhat," George pointed out, "and I think it would be safe for you to leave us for a while. I shall take good care of him."

"I can manage a short vacation if I am economical," John reflected.

George and Tom quickly agreed that their adored brother was to go off alone somewhere to finish his book, and the decision was for Burford Bridge, an out-of-the-way peaceful spot in Surrey that they had heard William Hazlitt mention more than once.

They'd keep in touch, of course, and as soon as they had

heard that his book was completed they would depart for Teignmouth, far south in the mild airs of the Devonshire coast, and John could join them there.

"We shall have a real holiday together!"

It was the middle of November 1817, when John Keats set out for Burford Bridge, a scant twenty-five miles to the south of London, over the road that passed through Epsom and Leatherhead. When he climbed down from the coach roof for the last time and stood in the dust, near the sweating, champing horses, a sudden wave of fatigue caused him to sway a bit unsteadily. But he found his way to the Fox and Hounds Inn, placing himself willingly in the care of the innkeeper.

"I'm giving you the room right next to the one occupied by Lord Nelson, sir," said the man, holding his lamp aloft to light Keats's way, "just before he set off for the Battle of Trafalgar."

In spite of his weariness, the twenty-two-year-old Keats found boyish delight in the thought. On occasion he had been Nelson himself, back in his sham-battling Enfield school days.

Keats took a late supper and went exhausted to bed, and when he awoke next morning he looked out upon pine and yew trees, gardens, and rolling country. He dressed hurriedly and dashed out of doors to discover that the village and inn stood in the valley of the meandering Mole River and all about were hills, hills, hills. As soon as he had had his tea he took a walk up the grassy slopes of Box Hill to have a better view of the countryside.

> O let me sip that tear!
> And whisper one sweet word that I may know
> This is this world—

This was indeed this world! He bolted back to his room, searched through his luggage for ink and pen and paper.

> Foot-feather'd Mercury appear'd sublime
> Beyond the tall tree tops . . .

His imagination was released from its inertia, and the verses began to appear one after another.

> So from the turf outsprang two steeds jet-black,
> Each with large dark blue wings upon his back . . .

and Endymion upon the back of one, his maiden on the other, soared up into space, "high as the eagles," earth-bound no more.

Here in these hills and dales Keats was experiencing a higher and higher level of creativity, richer thoughts were coursing through his mind, moving Endymion toward his great mystical conclusion.

Endymion could not absorb all the riches that John Keats possessed at that moment and so he shared the overflow with his friends—in letters—and in one of the loveliest of them he said,

"I am certain of nothing but the holiness of the heart's affections and the truth of imagination. What the imagination seizes as beauty must be truth, whether it existed before or not; for I have the same idea of all our passions as of love; they are all, in their sublime, creative of essential beauty."

CHAPTER VIII

Endymion

"I CANNOT GO with Tom into Devonshire," John Keats wrote to Reynolds on the twenty-second of November.

The decision to stay with his brothers so far from London had been made impulsively, and in the cool light of reflective reason he knew he could bear to be in only one part of England when his *Endymion* was being edited and printed and proofread. He had begun already to miss the trade gossip of London, in spite of the diligent letter-writing of his friends. What was "Blackguard's" up to? How was the Hunt–Haydon feud coming on? What was Leigh Hunt saying about his part in *Endymion*?

The last line of *Endymion* was written on the twenty-eighth of November:

                    Peona went
Home through the gloomy wood in wonderment.

The poet gathered his quills into an ink-stained bouquet and laid them gently away in a corner of his luggage, and beside

them he placed the neatly stacked pages of Book IV. Then
out he went himself through the wooded paths of Surrey "in
wonderment," in faith, in doubt. *Endymion* was truly a long
poem, four thousand and fifty lines, and for him it had been
a deep and important experience. Perhaps the public would
feel differently about it. Perhaps he himself would feel
differently about it after it had had time to grow cool and
he reread it. He hoped fervently that he would like it as it
was—would find it fresh, spontaneous, finished, or almost so.

He strode up the side of Box Hill and looked around him
at Surrey—lovely, peaceful, soul-releasing. How green would
this land be in the summer? Even now its pine and yew gave
it a verdant look. How would it seem after a gentle snowfall?
A pleasant inertia, end product of an important task completed, began to envelop him, and he decided to spend a few
more days—oh, perhaps even a week or two—in Burford
Bridge before returning to London.

But English days are shortest in December; the sun sets
around four and does not rise again until about eight. The
weather can be dark and foggy, or cold winds, driving sleet,
and heavy frost may happen, even to a poet.

> In a drear-nighted December,
>   Too happy, happy tree,
> Thy branches ne'er remember
>   Their green felicity:
>   The north cannot undo them
>   With a sleety whistle through them;
>   Nor frozen thawings glue them
>   From budding at the prime.
>
> In a drear-nighted December,
>   Too happy, happy brook,
> Thy bubblings ne'er remember
>   Apollo's summer look;
>   But with a sweet forgetting,

> They stay their crystal fretting,
> Never, never petting
> About the frozen time.

It was time to go home, John Keats decided very early in December; it was certainly time to go home. Tom and George would not have left for Teignmouth yet, and he could be there to see them off.

Tom was frankly disappointed and a little petulant over the fact that John had decided not to go to Devonshire with them, but George, unburdened by consumptive temperatures, took a more objective view of the situation. He would go with Tom—for a while—but John must remember about his engagement and wedding that was planned. Yes, yes, John remembered; he simply needed a few weeks to make final revisions on his manuscript, talk to Taylor and Hessey, and plan format.

On a penetrating cold day in the middle of December John Keats saw his two brothers aboard the long-distance stage.

"I'll join you as soon as I can," he promised.

The clatter of the horses hooves on the cobblestones had not died away before an elation began to well up in John Keats, an elation born of *Endymion*'s completion and acceptance by the publisher and an end of the poet's temporary isolation from his friends. He began to seek out his friends—all of them!—as though he had been away from London for years, thirsty for talk, for news, for the comradeship of creative, free-minded men. Off he went to the theater with Reynolds to see Shakespeare's *Richard III*. In another few days he was with Brown and Dilke watching a Christmas pantomime at Covent Garden.

He wrote long, reportorial letters to his brothers of his December days in London, and they could scarcely have been called drear.

John Keats, from the Joseph Severn miniature

Marble bust of John Keats by Malvina Hoffman

Fanny Brawne, from a contemporary
miniature

Sonnet in the handwriting of John Keats, from original manuscript
in The Pierpont Morgan Library

Endymion · Book 1st

A thing of beauty is a joy for ever:
Its loveliness increases; it will never
Pass into nothingness; but still will keep
A bower quiet for us, and a sleep
Full of sweet dreams, and health, and quiet breathing.
Therefore, on every morrow, are we wreathing
A flowery band to bind us to the earth,
Spite of Despondence, & of the inhuman dearth
Of noble natures, of the gloomy days,
Of all the unhealthy and oer-darkened ways
Made for our searching: yes, in spite of all
Some shape of beauty moves away the Pall
From our dark spirits. ~~and before us starting~~
~~Like glitter on the points of Gothic towers~~.
~~Of these bright powers are~~ Such the Sun, ~~and~~ the Moon
Trees old, and young sprouting a shady boon
For simple sheep; ~~of these~~ and such are daffodils
~~And~~ With the green world they live in; and clear rills
That for themselves a cooling covert make
'Gainst the hot season; the mid forest brake
Rich with a sprinkling of fair Muskrose blooms:
~~These~~ Aged & such is too are the grandeur of the dooms
We have imagined for the mighty dead;

Page 1 of the original manuscript of *Endymion* in The Pierpont
Morgan Library

John Keats at Wentworth Place by Joseph Severn

Leigh Hunt, from the portrait by Samuel Laurence

Joseph Severn as a young man, from the frontispiece in William
Sharp's *Life and Letters of Joseph Severn*, 1892

The house in Rome where John Keats died

"Severn tells me he has an order for some drawings for the Emperor of Russia. I was at a dance at Redhall's and passed a pleasant time enough. Drank deep and won 10.6 at cutting for Half Guineas."

He discovered when he dropped in at Haydon's studio that the huge painting of "Christ's Entry" was well advanced. His own head, above Voltaire's, was completed, and Haydon was working on one just below: Wordsworth's.

"The Wordsworth family has come up to London for a few weeks," Haydon told him, "and the poet is interested in meeting you. They are stopping in Lambeth. Can you go with me soon?"

Soon? Yes, yes! Keats was ready the moment that Haydon was, and in another day or two they were walking toward the Thames to cross into Lambeth, and Keats was gabbling in a sort of monologue about Wordsworth, boyishly trying to remember all he could about him. Wordsworth must be forty-seven or forty-eight by now; he'd once been deeply influenced by the French Revolution and Rousseau, had loved a French girl, and in his youth had been the same kind of brilliant radical as Keats, Hunt, Shelley. . . .

"I am convinced that there are three things to rejoice at in this age," said Keats to Haydon with a sudden flashing glance, "Wordsworth's *Excursion*, your pictures, and Hazlitt's depth of taste."

Haydon's ego burst into full blossom and he replied gallantly, "Allow me to add sincerely a fourth to be proud of— *John Keats's genius!*"

They were both in a marvelous frame of mind when they arrived at Wordsworth's. Their host was not ready for them, and so they sat primly in the parlor for quite a spell before he appeared. Keats could not help but stare as he rose slowly to his feet to be presented, for Wordsworth looked conservative enough to sit in the House of Lords. He was obviously dressed for a dinner party in snug breeches, silk stockings, a frock coat, a frilly shirt, and a silk cravat wound repeatedly around a high stiff collar. He sat with his two visitors long enough to exchange some conversation, and Haydon, just as conceited as Wordsworth and much bolder, persisted in his exalted opinion of Keats's poetry.

"What have you written lately?" Wordsworth asked Keats.

Haydon promptly answered for Keats, "He has written an exquisite 'Ode to Pan.' It is part of a long poem that he has just completed."

"Can you recite it for me?" Wordsworth asked.

Eagerly Keats jumped up to comply, pitching his low, rich voice to a modified chant, walking up and down during the recitation, his face alight. Haydon felt that he was hearing the young Apollo himself, but Wordsworth only commented dryly:

"A very pretty piece of paganism."

A remnant of the pugnacious schoolboy rose very close to the surface in Keats, but he managed not to reply. He and Haydon left soon after, and when they were out in the street Haydon indulged in some vituperative comments. Keats, hurt though he was, managed to keep silent for a few hundred paces, and then he said, "He is a great poet. I should like to know him better."

"You shall," Haydon promised him, and about a week later held a dinner party in his studio that has come down to us as "The Immortal Dinner."

To that dinner were invited John Keats, William Wordsworth, Thomas Monkhouse (who was Mrs. Wordsworth's cousin), John Landseer the painter and engraver, Charles Lamb, and a man named John Kingston, who was a Comptroller of the Stamp Office. Keats, ever sensitive to color, watched with secret amusement the constantly changing ef-

fect of the shifting candlelight on their faces. Wordsworth's
face had grown rather sharp and set and now and again his
prominent nose seemed to flutter. Keats had met Kingston
on another occasion and already thoroughly disliked him. The
yellowish light and undulating shadows on Kingston's face
showed him for what he was, a man whose manners and ideas
were standardized by acceptable fashions. Landseer was a
much more likable fellow, and Charles Lamb was someone
whom Keats had met at previous affairs and profoundly
admired. Lamb was a fellow romanticist, a lover of Shakespeare who, with his sister Mary, had written *Tales from
Shakespeare* for children. Lamb was a superb essayist, a
writer for *The Examiner*, a friend of the Novellos, a goer to
the theater. Lamb's sensitive, attractive face seemed spiritual
in candlelight.

Food and wine, in the usual Haydon tradition, were rich
and lavish, and conviviality developed quickly. Wordsworth
automatically assumed his role of prima donna, and in a pontif-
ical manner led the rapid-fire discussion of Homer, Shakespeare, Milton, and Virgil. Lamb, on the other hand, became
merry and witty and punctuated Wordsworth's solemn tones
with quip after quip, and Wordsworth took it all good-na-
turedly.

Keats, so recently returned to earth from his ethereal adventure with Endymion, knew tonight "that this is this
world," knew his place was with this circle of men as he kept
pace with their conversation, felt the edge of Wordsworth's
wounding comment about his poem become dulled and his
admiration for the man return by leaps and bounds. He sat
suddenly forward in his chair when he heard Lamb say to
Wordsworth:

"You old Lake Poet, you rascally poet, why do you call
Voltaire dull?"

Another round of rapid-fire conversation was touched off,

until at last Lamb raised his glass and gave a toast to "Voltaire, the Messiah of the French Nation."

Lamb stood up to give his toast, and Keats noticed that Lamb was weaving a bit, had in fact gone too deeply into his cups; and when they all left the table and sat about in an adjoining room with their tea, Lamb found himself a very comfortable chair near the fire, and his head was soon nodding.

Everyone had forgotten the Comptroller of Stamps, until suddenly, wanting desperately to go on record as an educated and cultured man but not daring to express a literary opinion in such brilliant company, he addressed a question to Wordsworth: "Don't you think, sir, Milton was a great genius?"

Keats looked in sudden amazement at Haydon, who began to study the ceiling. Wordsworth stared at the comptroller. Lamb lifted his head and asked,

"Pray, sir, did you say Milton was a great genius?"

"No, sir!" protested the comptroller. "I *asked* Mr. Wordsworth if he were not."

"Oh, then," Lamb told him, waving a limp hand. "Then you are a silly fellow."

To quell the laughter gathering within himself, Keats began to study Haydon's shelf of books with great intensity.

But the comptroller repeated himself wistfully, "Don't you think Newton a great genius?"

"Who *is* this?" Wordsworth wondered aloud.

Lamb jumped up, seized a candle, and approached the questioner. "Sir, will you allow me to look at your phrenological development?"

Then Charles Lamb began to dance about the room, candle in hand, reciting, "Diddle diddle dumpling, my son John." At each question from the comptroller he added a few more dance steps and another line of nursery rhyme, alternating between "My son John" and "The Cat and the Fiddle."

When the comptroller tried to make a joke out of his "cor-respondence" with Wordsworth, he being a comptroller of stamps, Lamb wove across the room toward him and held the candle close to his face to see wh-a-at-sort-fello-he-waas, and Keats and Haydon leaped to the rescue, each taking Lamb by an arm and guiding him back into the painting room. Shutting the door securely behind them, all three fell into chairs and laughed until tears ran down their cheeks and their sides ached.

Keats gave his brothers only a brief report of the evening in an otherwise long, news-packed letter, because he was be-ginning to feel pressed for time. He had begun his recopying of the *Endymion* manuscript, and was having one of his rare visits with his sister, who had been permitted to come up to London for the Christmas holidays.

"I have seen Fanny twice, lately," he wrote to George and Tom, who were still at Teignmouth, staying with a family named Jeffrey. "She has been unwell but is improving."

During this rare opportunity to gossip with his sister he told her about Tom's declining health, looking covertly all the while at her own spindle-limbed thinness.

"Are you sure Tom is getting proper care?" Fanny asked.

"Yes, I am; and I shall go to Teignmouth myself as soon as I can finish up here, and I shall send you a firsthand ac-count. They have had a doctor named William Turton."

He was making the promise to himself as well. Fanny had asked the question that haunted his own mind: was Tom getting good care? Tom seemed to think he was, and so did George, but John wanted to see for himself. He would, as soon as *Endymion* was in final form. On January 20, 1818, he took Book I of his manuscript to the publishers and settled down to copy the other three books, refreshing himself now and again by attending a series of lectures in literary criticism being given by William Hazlitt. He even jotted down an occasional idea for his next book-length poem, but just now in this interim period he could "only write in scraps and patches," he told his brothers.

One of his "scraps and patches" proved to be the poem, "Lines on Seeing a Lock of Milton's Hair," after an evening at Vale of Health when Hunt showed him the latest addition to his collection of locks of hair, an authentic bit clipped from Milton's venerable head.

He was receiving appeals from George and Tom to come to Devonshire. Tom wanted to see him, and George wanted to return to London and Georgiana, and he wrote to tell them just how far he had progressed: "I have given the first book to Taylor; he seemed more than satisfied with it, and to my surprise proposed publishing it in quarto if Haydon would make a drawing of some event therein for a frontispiece. I called on Haydon. He said he would do anything I liked. . . . I begin today to copy my second book. . . . Fanny has returned to Walthamstow . . ."

And to George and Tom during the middle of February: "The Wednesday before last Shelley, Hunt and I wrote each a sonnet on the River Nile. Some day you shall read them all. I saw a sheet of *Endymion* and have all reason to suppose they will soon get it done . . . I have been writing at intervals many songs and sonnets, and I long to be at Teignmouth to read them over to you. However, I think I had better wait till this book is off my mind . . ."

It was an irksome and frustrating time, that interim period between the finished manuscript and its appearance in print, a time filled with clerical chores, and Keats began to accumulate nervous tensions. A bout of sleeplessness set in. In the midst of it all he received a letter from George threatening to come home whether John came to Teignmouth or not, and even though George had been reporting Tom as "nearly in good health" and "much better" John could not bear the idea of Tom's being left alone so far away.

John wrote a hasty appeal to Clarke, asking him to take care of galley proofs that would be sent to him directly by Taylor and Hessey, gave the finished Book III to his publishers, and, packing the still unrecopied Book IV with a few items of clothing, hurried up to London in a gathering storm to catch an evening coach to Exeter.

He was growing so short of cash that in spite of the weather he rode on the roof. As the damp and cold penetrated his clothing, his bones ached and he sank slowly into a deep depression. The ride was long and wearing, and he did not reach Exeter until late morning of the next day. There he changed to a small, local vehicle that took him the last twelve-odd miles out to the coast and Teignmouth.

Teignmouth, the quaint little seaport, fishing town and resort on the mouth of the River Teign that his brothers had been extolling for the last several weeks, was being bathed by a steady drizzle of rain, and what scenery there may have been was hidden in a low-lying mist. Keats's physical strength was gone, but he forced himself to take the last few paces to find the house in the Strand where his brothers were stopping. The reunion was sudden and a little hysterical, and in stepping from the damp cold into the warm room and the company of the two men whom he loved "passing the love of women," Keats felt a compulsion to cry as hard as he had laughed at the "Immortal Dinner."

"I'll—need—a room—"

"You will have my half of this one," said George who was already packed for his return to Georgiana.

That night John Keats undressed and slid his exhausted limbs between the sheets of George's bed, and sleep began to engulf him almost at once while he reflected that Tom did look "much better," just as George had reported. Oh, he felt old—as old as King Lear—and as solemn—and seasoned by life—

On awaking many hours later he still felt seasoned. The now heavily falling rain sustained his solemnity, but his body felt lighter and younger. It must be morning, although the room seemed darkish. Tom was still asleep in the other bed. John arose quietly and went to the window, looking out into a street so narrow that it must have denied the little room any possible sunshine, if there ever was sunshine in Teignmouth. He rinsed his face at the washstand, decided to shave later, slipped into his clothes, and pulling Book IV out of his bag laid it on the table.

A gentle tap at the door caused Tom to open his eyes and turn his head.

"It's Marian," he told John.

Marian Jeffrey, quiet, sympathetic, in her 'teens, entered with their morning tea, and before the day was out John Keats had added to his list of friends Marian Jeffrey, her younger sister Sarah, and their widowed mother Margaret Jeffrey—the friendly, solicitous family about whom George and Tom had been telling him.

Later in the day Doctor Turton called, and John Keats was favorably impressed with his medical knowledge and understanding of consumption. They agreed optimistically—the two medical men—that Tom was on the road back to health. But when Dr. Turton looked hard at John, John stiffened a bit in his manner.

"Your cheek seems a bit feverish," the doctor observed. "Do try to remain in until the weather clears."

The weather did not clear for six days, and John Keats remained in a great deal during most of them, working intensively to complete Book IV. The rest of his time he spent reading *Endymion* to Tom, along with his other "scraps and pieces," and talking his soul out to Tom. Tom was eighteen, deeply mature in spirit and philosophy, capable of ethereal moods and departures, and the closest to himself in poetic kinship of anyone that he knew.

Keats was almost through with his manuscript before what he had come to call "the abominable Devonshire weather . . . splashy, rainy, misty, snowy, foggy, haily, floody, muddy, slipshod," began to ease, and he could stretch his limbs in a refreshing stride down the Strand to the "Den" or "Dene," a grassy promenade behind the beaches of the semicircular inlet on which Teignmouth stood. There he found crowds of promenaders as grateful for the change of weather as he. From it he had a fine view of the town's harbor, bristling with the masts of sailing vessels, their sails furled, others standing out to sea, and he could hear lively music coming from one of the town's public dance halls. Where the mist lifted he could see rolling green hills rising behind Teignmouth.

When he had had his fill of air, he hurried back to the little room and declared that Tom was to have a stroll with him tomorrow if the weather continued dry. And the weather did. The next day was lovely, even a bit sunny, and the two brothers awoke to it with picnic excitement, bundling themselves up for the adventure. They found the cliffs "a fine deep color" and the clouds "continually vying with them." Ecstatic to be out once more, Tom talked at great length about the walks and paths he and George had found in the meadows and hills and along the river, and John held his arm to restrain his pace.

"It is really much finer here than in Hampstead, John. Look! The primroses are out. Shall we go down on the beach? I think the sand is dry enough."

"Doctor" Keats decided against the additional exertion and persuaded his brother home and back to his bed for a rest, while he returned to the last pages of *Endymion*.

Tom's excitement changed gradually to nervous irritability during the day, and John found it almost impossible to work through the many interruptions and demands for attention. Tom lost all desire for food, and John went to the Jeffreys' kitchen to supervise the preparation of his tray, just as he had once done for his mother, but on returning he found Tom in a jealous sulk at the time he'd spent with the Jeffrey women.

"I heard you laughing!"

That was true enough. Marian and Sarah were full of fun, and a lot of flirting had gone on during the winter between them and the Keats brothers.

As the day waned John lit candles and concentrated on *Endymion*, but suddenly sensing something he looked at his brother. Tom lay watching him with overbright eyes, and said, "I'm sorry, John."

A sudden fit of coughing brought Tom to a sitting position, shaking and racking his frame, and John threw down his pen and rushed to Tom's side, holding him in his arms until the attack subsided. The cough changed to a muffled choking and blood flowed from Tom's mouth, staining his lips and chin and the palms of his hands. John looked horrified at the symptom.

> darkness, death and darkness.
> Even here, into my centre of repose,
> The shady visions come to domineer . . .

Holding Tom with one arm, he piled pillows behind him so that he would not have to lie flat, and Tom sank back into deep, despairing exhaustion. Outside the rainfall had begun again.

John managed to finish *Endymion* and post it to London, returning to his table to seek spiritual release in letters, letters, letters. He first wrote to George telling him of the change for the worse in Tom's condition, then to Bailey, Reynolds, and Haydon. They were long letters, full of philosophic reflections and verses.

He received a prompt reply from George, expressing his surprise at the change in Tom's health, urging him not to let Tom "presume on his strength" again, assuring John that he was in touch with Taylor and Hessey, and enclosing a much needed twenty pounds.

Their decision was to keep Tom in Teignmouth until spring weather reached London and until he was strong enough for the return journey. Tom had to remain in bed altogether, and generously Marian Jeffrey came up to alternate with John in nursing him.

"Stay till the summer," Haydon wrote back, "and then bask in its deep blue summer sky, and lush grass, and tawny banks, and silver bubbling rivers. You must not leave Devonshire without seeing some of its scenery—rocky, mossy, craggy with roaring rivers and as clear as crystal . . . Shakespeare in speaking of somebody who is gradually dying makes one say, 'How is he?' 'Still ill, nature and sickness debate it at their leisure'. Is this not exquisite? When I die I'll have my Shakespeare placed on my heart, with Homer in my right hand and Ariosto in the other, Dante under my head, Tasso at my feet and Corneille under my—I hate that Corneille!"

John Keats had to laugh when he read that, in spite of his depressing assignment. He'd get through the next few weeks, he knew, with news-packed letters coming to him from such friends as this.

And there was still a Preface to be written for *Endymion* . . .

Once more Tom progressed toward health, although an occasional minor hemorrhage set him back. During April the heavy rainfall persisted, but John Keats did manage to do some exploring on foot during the dry days. On one very beautiful afternoon he had "a fine clamber over the rocks"; on another he "found a lane banked on each side with store of primroses, while the earlier bushes are beginning to leaf."

Cast so utterly and unexpectedly upon his own resources in those March and April weeks, he did the thing most natural to a writer to save himself from his own unavoidable situation; he wrote a narrative poem based on one of the tales from Boccaccio's *Decameron*. Nostalgically, he called it "Isabella, or, the Pot of Basil," using almost automatically the theme of death. Isabella and Lorenzo were young lovers, separated when Isabella's brothers murdered him and buried his body in a nearby forest. Isabella found the body, brought home the head, and hid it in a pot of basil. The ghoulish story was a departure from the profuse richness of *Endymion*, and its eight-line stanzas and rhyme scheme (abababcc) a deliberate Italianism.

Toward the end of April he received by post a treasure for which he waited, an advance copy of *Endymion*, and he tore open the wrappings and sat down close to Tom so that they could study the volume together. It was a larger, handsomer volume than *Poems*, its untrimmed pages 5⅝ by 8¾ inches, its boards the same light brown color, and the title page reading, "Endymion: A Poetic Romance by John Keats." Earlier plans for a larger format and a Haydon illustration had been abandoned.

John began to read the book through for errata, making a careful tabulation of some fourteen or fifteen.

"I think I did very wrong to leave you to all the trouble of *Endymion*," he wrote to John Taylor when he forwarded the errata. "But I could not help it then . . . The book pleased me much. It is very free from faults . . ."

Tom had begun to declare himself well enough to travel, and the arrival of his brother's second book gave him so much vicarious pleasure that he felt doubly improved. Desperately eager to be home himself—for *Endymion* reviews, for George's wedding—John consented to the journey, and took Tom back to Hampstead by easy stages, stopping to rest at such towns as Honiton in Devonshire and Bridgport in Dorset. But at that second stop Tom experienced another hemorrhage, and a delay was necessary. The trip took nearly a week.

Not until he had placed Tom in bed at Well Walk was John Keats able to plunge back into his literary-social life, making an early call on his publishers. Taylor and Hessey's legal adviser, Richard Woodhouse, was most enthusiastic about *Endymion*.

"I really consider it superior to some of Shakespeare's very early things," he said with absolute sincerity.

George Keats was delighted about *Endymion*, too, but his wedding was only three weeks off, his trip to America an established certainty, and his attention was really taken up by Georgiana and the 1,400 acres in Kentucky that he had purchased from the United States government.

In spite of John's determination to give George a cheerful time of it during these last days, his spirits were sinking under the pressure of having to realize that he was losing George and could lose Tom.

"I am now so depressed that I have not an idea to put to paper," he wrote to Bailey. "I feel no spur at my brother's going to America and am almost stony-hearted about his wedding."

George knew his own brother, and he knew what a blow he was dealing him.

"Let's have one devilish evening as bachelors while we can," George proposed only a few days before his wedding. "What do you say to the Lyceum Theatre tonight?"

John leaped at the suggestion and a trace of his gaiety came back as they indulged themselves by riding up to London and at George's insistence went to a favorite inn for a festive dinner.

"Shall it be the breast of a partridge, the back of a hare, the backbone of a grouse, the wing and side of a pheasant?" asked the poet in a sudden surge of happiness.

"Oh, I hope they have some game bird tonight, and a fine white French wine."

They emerged from the inn into the dark street, rendered more shadowy than light by the flickering street lamps. Feeling a little stouter they walked at a moderate pace toward the Strand. On a sudden impulse John seized George's arm with one hand and pointed ahead of them toward the approaching figure of a woman with the other.

"There she is!"

"Who?"

"My lady from Hastings!" John declared, and shouted to her, "Isabella! Isabella!"

But George caught his arm and pulled him back before John could run up to her.

"Keep quiet and stay here, you fool!" he hissed into John's ear. "Can't you see she's with an escort?"

"Oh, he's stout and bald. He must be her father."

"Wait and see if she wants to acknowledge you."

John forced himself to a gentlemanly pace, pulse racing wildly, and waited intently for the recognition that came.

"Oh, it is Mr. John Keats," she said, smiling and nodding down at them from the top of a mountain peak.

"And this is my brother, George Keats," John replied as he took her hand.

She presented them both to her companion, Mr. O'Callaghan, and in another minute the meeting was ended.

Old bald-pate . . . old man . . . I want no light in the dusk, no torch in the gloom . . . but my Isabel's eyes . . . and her lips . . .

CHAPTER IX

Let Me Begin My Dream

JOHN COULD NEVER have told what the opera at the Lyceum was that night. All he could think about was the question that had almost died, or at least had been reduced to quiescence, now raised once more: Was he in love with Isabella Jones? He could have talked it out with George had his brother's mind and heart not been so filled with his impending marriage.

His spirits sank once more

> Deep in the shady sadness of a vale
> Far sunken from the healthy breath of morn . . .

and reached their lowest point on the morning that he sat next to Tom and among their other friends in the darkened interior of a church to witness the marriage of Georgiana Wylie and George Keats. The church bells overhead tolling their "melancholy round" and the finality of the statements intoned by the presiding clergy reminded him of his mother's funeral. He felt a little sickish and his throat was slightly sore when he swallowed, but at the time he rather thought that his depressed state of mind was responsible for his physical condition.

In another few days he was genuinely ill, and the local doctor forbade him to leave the house. A fine pair they were, he and Tom, hiding from the air, the rain, the mists. Thank heaven for the friends who came to visit them.

"I could not live without the love of my friends," was John Keats's reflection.

Joseph Severn walked across the fields from smoky London to Well Walk with candid delight, and declared he came to profit by the brightness of Keats's genius. His excuse for coming, he added, was to paint a miniature portrait of Keats.

"I really come for the pleasure of your company," he said with genuine humility. "That is my real excuse for obtruding my miniature self on your superior company."

But at this point the most attentive and most concerned friend was Charles Armitage Brown. Brown saw the combination of circumstances pulling Keats's spirit down, the false hope created every time Tom showed signs of improvement, the despair every time he spit up blood. And he knew how deeply the worry over reviews of *Endymion* was gnawing at Keats. Favorable reviews appeared in one or two minor publications, and Leigh Hunt was keeping silent so that Keats's second book would not be damned by its association with him and *The Examiner*. The volume was dedicated to the memory of a long-dead poet, Thomas Chatterton. The two most influential and most-to-be-feared magazines, *Blackwood's* and the *Quarterly*, were yet to be heard from. And there was a third Tory paper, *The British Critic*. The combination of these three—still ranting about "The Cockney School"—could kill *Endymion*.

Keats had recently protested to Reynolds that he did not

care for "mawkish popularity," but Brown knew that if Keats were hovering on the brink of death he would not die until he had read those reviews. Dweller-on-the-surface though he was himself, Brown saw the depths and heights of Keats's genius as clearly as men like Haydon, Hunt, and Severn saw it, knew the sensitivity of his soul, and realized how deeply he would suffer if those critics attacked him.

Earlier in the spring Keats and Brown had talked of going on a walking tour through northern England and Scotland, and Brown raised the subject again. It appealed to Keats immediately, and they asked Severn to make it a trio.

"I don't have the funds," Severn told them. "And I don't think it would be wise for me to leave town now."

He was doing rather well painting miniature portraits, and he knew that if he were out of sight of his clients and their word-of-mouth advertising for long he would be out of their minds too.

"I think I can get some funds from Abbey," Keats said.

"You shall go with me whether funds come from Abbey or no," Brown declared with implicit confidence in that Englishman's panacea: a long walk in the country.

Keats had as much faith in the northern tour as Brown. It would raise his spirits, clear away that feverish, congested feeling, and the slightly toxic, depressed, insomnious state he had sunk into. Tom was really well enough, and the Baileys had promised to look after him—and there was Mrs. Dilke.

So plans were made. As soon as John had seen George and Georgiana off to America, he and Brown could set out. The two hikers and the bride and groom all boarded the stage for Liverpool on June 22, 1818. For Keats it was a prologue to the kind of life he intended to pursue, "to write, to study and to see all of Europe at the lowest expense." He would "clamber to the clouds and exist." He would rather have struck out for greater distances, to Athens and the ancient mountains of Greece, to Italy where there could be a hope of meeting Byron, or to the *moon*, but Scotland would do for the present. Abbey had credited his account with five hundred pounds earlier in the month to take care of both Tom and himself, and had sent him another hundred and seventy just before his departure.

In the long carriage ride the four talked of their plans. Keats and Brown were to be gone for at least four months. John estimated that he would be able to come to America to visit George in about three years.

They reached the Crown Inn in Liverpool in time for their evening meal on the second day and, aching in every bone, went early to bed. John Keats and Brown were up long before the George Keatses and took another stage northward to the city of Lancaster, the proposed starting point of their tour. Lancaster was a busy town, on the verge of an election, and no treat to two men bent on escaping from London. Whigs and Tories argued loudly in the streets and around inn tables; inn rooms were all taken; spirits flowed so freely that troops were being held in readiness in case of trouble. Keats and Brown looked at each other in despair, and deciding that one inn was as bad as another walked into the handiest for dinner. In the smoky room crowded with tipsy, shouting customers, they waited two hours to be served.

"Thank heaven this is the last big town on our route," said Brown when they were finally able to leave.

They charmed their way into a room in a private home for the night, determined to be on their way at four in the morning. But when they awoke at four they did not need to look out of the window to know that it was pouring.

"It can't last forever."

"Oh, no. It is bound to stop."

They dressed and repacked their knapsacks—socks, underwear, razors, soap, alternate shirt, oilskin capes, Dante's *Di-*

vine Comedy, Milton's poems, pens, ink, and paper for Keats —Brown kept out the copy of Milton and with one eye on the weather began to read aloud from *Samson Agonistes*. The rain poured down and Brown read on—for three hours—and then the two discouraged travelers convinced themselves that what was falling was by now only a Scotch mist and they started out—Keats in a fur cap, jacket and trousers, with a plaid tartan around his shoulders; Brown in a white hat, tartan coat, an extra tartan over his shoulders, and spectacles that frequently needed to have the mist removed.

As Keats trudged over the slippery wet cobblestones and across the bridge of the Lune River, he felt deeply relieved to be on the road and free of city confusions and crowds, his holiday begun at last. He was grateful for a companion who knew when to keep silent, a time like now when the country was a deep, soft green, the air filled with a brackish tang because of the tidal bay they were skirting. Miraculously they had the world to themselves for an hour of walking until they came to the hamlet of Bolton-le-Sands. They were famished! They strode into an inn and ordered large breakfasts. As they ate the rain began to come down in torrents again.

"Will it stop soon, do you think?" they asked the local weather prophets.

Heads shook; mouths turned down. But the prophets were wrong. By noon the skies cleared, leaving only a mist along the horizons, and the hikers were off again.

Two miles beyond Bolton the road curved gently and gave them a marvelous view of the hilly countryside, and soon they had reached Burton-in-Kendal. Famished again! With no more than a look of agreement exchanged, they dashed for the Green Dragon Inn. But they were stopped by a huge, homely, ill-tempered innkeeper.

"You can have nothing here!"

"It's the green dragon himself," declared Brown.

"But we need dinner," put in Keats.

His inn was filled with soldiers brought in to keep order during the coming election, the green dragon explained. They went on to the King's Arms, and were told, "The soldiers are upon us," but the landlady was willing to serve them a meal.

The rain had begun again, and Keats decided to wear his oilskin cape. Brown did likewise. Farther along the road they came to a rather sorry-looking public house.

"It should be dry inside," Keats observed.

The landlady was sucking a large dirty pipe and emitting puffs of dark smoke.

"I'm full," she said. "Go on to End Moor."

Keats was beginning to feel that he'd done sufficient walking, but they had to go on until they found refuge for the night. When they did it was in the deteriorated home of a pensioned soldier and his wife, after convincing the couple that they weren't peddlers.

They had covered seventeen miles that day, and when Keats slipped between the coarse sheets, too tired to question their cleanliness, he shivered for quite a while before his body heat warmed up the bedding around him. What good company Brown was, he reflected, much better than he had had any idea.

Early next morning they tramped on to Kendal in fine weather, had breakfast there, and—filled with verve—set out to walk the next nine miles to Bowness on Lake Windermere. Keats was increasing his rate of speed somewhat, because reaching Lake Windermere meant the beginning of the Lake District, land of the Lake Poets. To the north of this first lake, some seven miles above Bowness, was Rydal Mount, Wordsworth's home.

The road began to rise through a slow incline and curve

to the west; they were "getting among the hills and to see mountains grow up before" them. Suddenly they came out upon a rise, and the view caused them both to stop and stare in wonderment. Below them lay Bowness on the edge of the lake, typical hamlet of the region, a cluster of small one-story houses of gray stone with shallow-peaked roofs, a church among them, and the White Lion Inn conspicuous because it was a story taller. Beyond the village to the north and south stretched the great Lake of Windermere, the Winander Mountains to the north, "beautiful water, shores and islands green to the marge, mountains all round up to the clouds."

"How can I believe that?" asked Keats. "Surely it cannot be!"

He had been reading about mountains; he had written about mountains; now he was beholding them.

They hurried down the hill to the inn. It was dinner time; they had come fourteen miles; it felt good to relax into chairs at an inn table and have a leisurely meal of fresh lake trout. Keats pulled paper, pen, and ink out of his knapsack and spread them on the table, because he was keeping a detailed record of his trip in letters to George, Tom, and Fanny.

After dinner they set out again, walking another five miles along the rim of the lake to Ambleside. The "road was a winding lane, wooded on each side, and green overhead, full of foxgloves—every now and then a glimpse of the lake . . . large hills nestled together in a sort of gray black mist." Brown, too, was keeping a diary, and the day drew some poetic prose from him: "The country was wild and romantic, the weather fine, though not sunny, while the fresh mountain air, and many larks about us, gave us unbounded delight."

That night they put up at the Salutation Inn at Ambleside, and John Keats finished his records by candlelight.

"Tomorrow," he said, half to himself, as he was about to

fall asleep, "we shall reach Rydal Mount."

After breakfast, following a path through a deep valley, they walked to Wordsworth's home. It was an ample house that stood back from the road, half hidden behind aged shrubbery, and up on a ridge of land that gave it a view of the water to the south. Unconcerned that they looked like ragamuffins, since they were calling on a poet, John Keats and Charles Armitage Brown mounted the fifteen or more shallow stone steps up the rise of ground to the entrance. The premises were graced with stone walks and terraces embanked with field stones, and the seasoned old house was partly covered with ivy. A servant admitted them to a foyer where a wide stairway swept up to the second floor. She guided them past it into a low-ceilinged living room.

No, Mr. Wordsworth was not at home today, not at all, nor any other member of his family. He was out in a nearby town campaigning for the Tory candidate. It was a two-edged disappointment, missing the senior poet of the Romantic Movement, and being reminded that the man who had once been so bohemian was now an ultra-conservative.

"I wrote a note for him," Keats put into his letter to George, "and stuck it up over what I knew must be Miss Wordsworth's portrait. . . . I have had a great confidence in your being well able to support the fatigue of your journey since I have felt how much new objects contribute to keep off a sense of ennui and fatigue . . ."

John Keats was traveling on nervous excitement in part; his mild sore throat was still mildly sore; and while fourteen miles on a walking tour was "not so much as the four from Hampstead to London," the exhilaration of interest that carried him through each day's hike had begun to leave him at night overspent and overweary.

From Ambleside they went deeper into the wild countryside of the Lake District, through towns with ancient names

like Ireby and Wigton, to the modest city of Carlisle with
its ancient castle of sandy red stone and "old white washed
narrow streets, broad red brick ones more modern," almost
at the Scottish border. The mountains were behind them,
and the land around Carlisle and Solway Firth was quite flat.

"We have now walked 114 miles and are merely a little
tired in the thighs and a little blistered," John wrote to Tom.
"We shall ride thirty-eight miles to Dumfries."

That coach ride took them into Scotland on the first of
July, and a fellow passenger pointed out the tomb of Robert
Burns.

"There de ye see it, amang the trees; white, wi a round tap."

There was time that same afternoon to visit the tomb, and
John Keats expressed his disappointment in it and in the
poverty-stricken countryside—barefoot women walking along
the road, "wretched cottages where smoke has no outlet but
the door"—with his sonnet, "On Visiting the Tomb of Burns."

Another week of walking among the towns, hamlets, fields,
and crag hills along the Irish Sea brought them to Port Patrick
on the narrow channel that separates Scotland from Ireland.

"My dear Tom," Keats wrote from Ballantrae on the
tenth of July, "When we left Cairn our road lay half way
up the sides of a green mountainous shore, full of clefts of
verdure and eternally varying—sometimes up, sometimes
down, and over little bridges going across green chasms of
moss rock and trees—winding about everywhere. After two
or three miles of this we turned suddenly into a magnificent
glen finely wooded in parts— seven miles long—with a mountain stream winding down the midst—full of cottages in the
most happy situations—the sides of the hills covered with
sheep. The effect of cattle lowing I never had so finely. At
the end we had a gradual ascent and got among the tops of
the mountains whence in a little time I described in the sea
Ailsa Rock, 940 feet high . . ."

The sight of the "craggy ocean-pyramid" touched off another sonnet.

They resumed their walk toward Glasgow along the southern shore of the Firth of Clyde, and now John Keats was a poet on a pilgrimage to the shrine of a poet.

"I am approaching Burns's Cottage very fast . . . I had no conception that the native place of Burns was so beautiful . . . Every fantasy of green in tree, meadow, and hill . . ."

Brown caught the Burns fever from Keats, and they chatted with local residents all along the way, straining to understand the heavy dialect. Aye, here was the brig that Tam O'Shanter crossed, and here at Alloway was the thatched cottage where Burns was born. But at the cottage the two men found themselves immediately the victims of a talkative, stupid caretaker, filled with rehearsed humor and anecdotes. Keats and Brown exchanged a glance and tried to absorb the spirit of the place without hearing the banter.

"Is there no putting the fellow off?" Keats whispered at the first opportunity.

"I'm afraid not."

Keats did not want to leave without having written some lines in the cottage, and he did manage his sonnet, "Written in Burns' Cottage."

But once outside again he exploded angrily to Brown, "O the flummery of [the] birth place! Cant! Cant! Cant! It is enough to give a spirit the guts-ache . . . his gab hindered my sublimity. The flat dog made me write a flat sonnet."

Brown did not agree about the flatness of the sonnet, and we have it today because he made a copy at the first opportunity. He knew the dissatisfied Keats would destroy the original.

By the time they entered Glasgow on the evening of the thirteenth, Keats had forgotten his "flatness." The populous and busy gray stone city offered too much that other busy crowded places had, and so they left it early next day and set out toward Loch Lomond.

Keats almost despaired of his solitude when he saw that the long, lovely lake, set amidst the rich green hills, was beset with tourists—steamboats on the lake, barouches along its sides. They pushed on to the port of Oban.

Keats was driving himself a little harder each day. The farther north they went, the less often they found comfortable quarters at night. Now and again they stopped in a flea-infested room; gadflies tormented them; the food became more and more dismal until it was nothing but eggs and oatcake.

"I feel it a little," he confessed to Tom.

Yet, the marvelous scenery kept luring them on. Loch Awe was "a streak of water deep in the bases of large black mountains." Keats and Brown went on past lofty hills and deeply wooded steeps. But the lush, green coloring of the countryside was due to ample precipitation, and they walked the last fifteen miles to Oban in a pouring rain. From Oban they had planned to follow the chain of long, narrow lakes that almost divides Scotland in two between Oban and Inverness, but next day they dallied because it was still raining.

John Keats had caught a traveler's vision of the mystery beyond the horizon, of the joy the eyes can find in seeing something new and strange and a little farther away every day; and he had caught a sense of that subtle freedom in a lengthening road behind him. The lingering at Oban meant chatting with local men at inn tables about the region and the Hebrides Islands lying off the western shore of Scotland. Keats looked at Brown; Brown smiled; and with a guide they were ferried across in an oversized rowboat, first to the small island of Kerrera and then to the much larger island of Mull. On Mull they set out on the most strenuous hike of their trip so far. Keats knew in his heart that he was

expecting too much of himself as he clambered over miles
of heath and rock and sloshed, stockings in hand, through
river and bog. That night he slept in his clothes on the clay
floor of a shepherd's cottage, smoke from the fire burning his
eyes because there was no chimney. Next day he awoke with
a heavy cold and a severely sore throat, and still he could
not change his course. He continued the tour with Brown
"in a missling rain and splashy way," thirty-seven miles in
all.

The walking tour had become a kind of obsession in his
mind, like a long, long poem that had to be completed, and
there was more to be done, more, more, more. When he
and Brown returned to the mainland they followed their
original plan along the lakes to Inverness.

> There is a charm in footing slow across a silent plain,
> Where patriot battle has been fought, when glory had the
>   gain;
> There is a pleasure on the heath where Druids old have been,
> Where mantles grey have rustled by and swept the nettles
>   green;
> There is a joy in every spot made known in times of old,
> New to the feet, although each tale a hundred times be told;
> There is a deeper joy than all, more solemn in the heart,
> More parching to the tongue than all, of more divine a smart,
> When weary steps forget themselves upon a pleasant turf,
> Upon hot sand, or flinty road, or sea-shore iron scurf,
> Toward the castle or the cot, where long ago was born
> One who was great through mortal days, and died of fame
>   unshorn.

Keats was on a quest for education, the kind of education
a poet must have, the kind offered by "light heather-bells,"
woodlarks singing from sandy fern, green nettles, black
mountain peaks, blue tides sluicing and drenching their time

in caves and weedy creeks, eagles soaring wingwide upon the air.

The highest mountain peak in Great Britain was ahead of them: Ben Nevis, near Fort William.

"We must climb it," said Keats. "We passed up Helvellyn, and our climb up Skiddaw was scarcely an achievement."

"Do you feel well enough?" asked the doubtful Brown.

Oh, yes! His throat was not nearly so sore as it had been. He must surely be on the mend.

So, at five o'clock in the morning on the second of August, they set out from their inn at Fort William to hike and climb for seven-and-a-half miles up and the same distance back. With them went a guide in a tartan shawl and cap, a dog at his heels. There was a poem at the top waiting for Keats, and he had to capture it.

"After much fag and tug and a rest," he and Brown gained the first rise, and for the next mile their way lay along a heath valley and past a lake, but the ascent for the next three miles was rigorous and stony.

As they achieved altitude a mist settled around them and obscured their view, and they struggled and labored over fields of large, loose stones. Keats and Brown were both breathing hard to keep up with their wiry, tireless guide, who must have been born of a piece of Scottish granite instead of a human mother. Keats's throat grew dry and raspy and his chest felt tight. The air became colder, and patches of snow appeared on the ground, and when they were nearly at the top they passed a deep chasm filled with snow. A sharp wind whipped around them, and Keats fastened his jacket closer about himself. Walking now erect, now on all fours, now bent over their sticks, they at last reached the summit.

Where was the view? Where was the valley, the world below? They were wrapped in a cloud, but the same wind that had tugged at Keats's jacket gradually wafted the cloud away, and blue patches of sky began to show.

Keats's fatigue vanished as he stood and gazed at the panorama all around him, the wide green valley far below, other mountain peaks in the distance, Fort William looking like a miniature town. Taking a tablet from his pocket he perched on a rock near the edge of an almost vertical precipice, and wrote his sonnet, "Ben Nevis."

But his fatigue returned in a rush when he and Brown began their descent, and Keats slogged and trudged along, hoping that his strength would last long enough to get him back to Fort William. By the time they reached the inn, Keats was leaning heavily on Brown's arm, fighting for the last few steps. Brown helped him into bed and as Keats closed his eyes the room swelled and rocked and turned slowly about him. When he opened them again, he realized that Brown had fetched a doctor. Good old Brown!

"You are too thin and fevered to proceed farther," said the doctor. "Rest a few days here."

Keats gradually recovered sufficient energy to resume the walk to Inverness, sixty-six miles away, but it was a slow, slow trip, with stops at Invergarry and Inverfarigaig. He was able to do it only because he had fixed his mind on Inverness as a goal. Once there, he dismissed any idea of attempting to complete the last lap of their journey, Inverness to Edinburgh, and Brown inquired for boat services to London.

"There's a smack from Cromarty that stops here on August 8th," he came back and reported. It was already the sixth.

They had walked 642 miles together, and day by day their friendship had deepened, in long intimate hours of silence, in experiences shared—"we have been taken for spectacle venders, razor sellers, jewellers, travelling linen drapers, spies, excisemen"—and in reading and thinking aloud together. Keats did not want to leave Brown, but he could not say anything to deter his friend from finishing his walking tour, and he went aboard the smack alone.

Once the last good-by had been waved and the sailing vessel stood out to sea, Keats sank into a deck chair. It would take him nine days to reach London and Hampstead and Tom.

As his fatigue subsided and he managed several hours' sleep each night, his imagination began to relive the richness of the past few weeks: "thunderous waterfalls . . . crag jutting forth to crag . . . couches of rugged stones . . . Druid stones upon a forlorn moor . . . chill rain . . . sombre cliff . . . forest-trees . . . pale solitary doves . . . eagles golden-feather'd." A poet must seek eternally for his images as a bird seeks for choicest bits and pieces to weave a perfect nest. A poet must reach out wider and wider, higher and higher, to the gods, to their thunderous fathers. "Titans, behold!" Keats felt his brain running wild again, replenished by his journeyings; he felt his body recovering, relaxed by the rocking motion of the boat. Hyperion the Titan, father of the sun and the moon, walked through "moments big as years."

Keats left the boat at London Bridge and went straight out to Well Walk without stopping to see anyone in town. He was startled to be greeted by Dilke.

"Keats, my dear fellow, did you get my letter at Inverness?"

No; the letter had missed him.

It was Tom, Dilke explained. Tom had had a relapse, deuced serious.

John Keats rushed past him and up the stairs, stopping abruptly at the threshold to Tom's room, head spinning from panic and a fleeting vision of his mother in the face of the boy in the bed. Tom's eyes glistened and seemed overlarge because his face was so wasted; his body scarcely showed beneath the covers.

John Keats moved back into the sick room, ignoring the advice of friends that he live apart from his brother. He could have done it in no other way. Tom needed both medical and nursing care, and he was the person best qualified. Tom must be bled properly; his diet must be carefully restricted; his bodily needs must be lovingly served.

Added to the shock of discovering Tom's worsened condition was the news that the Tory press was launching a virulent attack on *Endymion*. *The British Critic* had struck the first blow in its June issue, indulging in stupid ridicule, grossly misrepresenting the story of *Endymion*, calling the poem "mawkish" and "a flimsy veil of words," a work filled with "immoral images," "better adapted to the stews." In its August issue *Blackwood's* published an ugly article on Keats and Hazlitt. It called *Endymion* driveling idiocy and the treatment of the ancient legend a "sickly fancy"; its author, said the article, was just "a cockney rhymester," a "starved apothecary," who would do better with pills and ointment boxes. In September a much delayed April issue of the *Quarterly Review* appeared, combining its efforts with the *Critic* and *Blackwood's* to ring the death knell for *Endymion*. The poem was unreadable, it said; its author lacking in powers of language and fancy and merely Leigh Hunt's simple neophyte.

Sitting at Tom's bedside, Keats could only wait for the pain and discouragement to wear away. Perhaps *Endymion was* a slipshod result; even an admirer of it had said that it contained "many passages indicating haste and carelessness," but he really could not have helped it. "It is as good as I had power to make it," he wrote to his publishers. "Had I been nervous about its being a perfect piece, and with that view asked advice, and trembled over every page, it would not have been written." All a writer could do was to begin by forgiving himself and go on to his next project, and from that project to the next and the next, hoping to reach a higher plane with each effort.

There was a peculiar peace in the enforced quiet of the sick room in which he ought to have been able to work, free of the whirl and wearing events outside. But the language would not flow and the words would not marshal. Ideas escaped, divided, eluded him like mercury. Hyperion would not live and breathe. Keats turned to Milton, then tried to come back to his writing. This failing, he read Ronsard. But in the silence he was watching Tom die, and the sight stifled and strangled creation; he was obliged to lay down his pen or book and go out at times to ease himself of Tom's "countenance, his voice and feebleness."

Tom needed cheering, he reflected, and he decided to try to obtain Abbey's permission for Fanny to come and visit. To his own surprise he did succeed, naïvely hoping that Fanny's presence would improve Tom's condition. But Fanny, an adolescent fifteen, emotional, and quite unprepared for the advanced state of Tom's illness, filled up at the first glimpse of her brother. Her lips trembled, her eyes brimmed over, and she rushed across the room and flung herself on top of him, choking and sobbing. Tom, reading his own destiny in her face, began to cry like a child.

Feeling suddenly wretched himself, John Keats strove to calm them both, without much effect, and when at last Fanny left he realized that his patient's condition had been worsened.

"Do let me come and see him again, John," Fanny begged as he assisted her down the stairs. "I promise you I won't go on so another time. It was just that I had no notion. Oh, John!" her voice broke again, and fresh tears appeared, "Are we going to lose Tom?"

"I don't know, but I shall try to bring you here again. It depends upon Abbey. I shall keep after the fat codger."

There was one more thing she wanted to talk to her oldest

brother about. The Abbeys wanted to take her out of that school, and she liked it there. John would do what he could about that, too, he promised, but she must remember that Abbey was within his right and too stupid to understand the joy of books and the company of fellow scholars.

John himself yearned for the company of fellow scholars. From the time of his return in August, all during the fall and into the beginning of winter, he spent most of his time with Tom, seeking no pleasures, seeing very few of his friends.

"I have been but once to Haydon's, once to Hunt's . . . once to Hessey's. I have not seen Taylor . . . I have not been to the theatre," he wrote to George. Occasionally he found his way to the Dilkes and Brown at Wentworth Place.

On one of his rare trips up to London he did have a brief encounter with Hazlitt and walked with him as far as Covent Garden, chatting fast to catch up. When he and Hazlitt parted company, Keats turned northward to Bedford Row and then into the street that would lead him into Lamb's Conduit Street. Suddenly his thoughts were interrupted by an impression that found its way to his consciousness slowly. He had passed someone! He wheeled about.

"Isabella!"

There she was again—and alone—and this time when she held out her hand to him there was a warm intimacy in her manner.

"I *am* glad to see you, John."

"Please forgive me for passing you by, Isabella."

"Oh, I was not offended."

> The shut rose shall dream of our loves and awake
> Full-blown, and such warmth for the morning's take . . .

"I am on my way to a girls' boarding school run by a friend of mine," she was saying. "If it does not inconvenience you why not come with me."

Eagerly he accompanied her on her walk through several more streets to a formal call in the parlor of a girls' school. Throughout the dull and proper conversation he stole glances at her, feeling a little disconcerted by the thought that without the benefit of sea air and wind burn, or the subdued lighting of a London street in the evening, she was older than he had realized. What of that, he argued with himself. What of that? It was the *soul* that counted. Soul and spirit!

"Now you must let me see you home!" he insisted, and she consented graciously.

They strolled all the way back into the heart of London and out Oxford Street to 34 Gloucester Street, Queen Square, thence upstairs to her sitting room. Keats was startled at the affluence of the place and at the indications of culture: books, original paintings, bronzes, an aeolian harp.

While I kiss to the melody, aching all through!

Impulsively he moved toward her, but she caught his wrists and guided him to a chair. But he had warmed to her and kissed her at Hastings, and not to do so now would be living backward!

"Our moment in Hastings was a happy one, but that was Hastings, and this is London," was her cryptic explanation.

To fill the tender breach she produced a bottle of excellent liqueur, and as they sipped it from the rims of fragile glasses the conversation was slowly reborn, until they were chatting gayly and Keats, the poet who so needed to think in torrents upon the air, was telling her of his family, George's marriage and departure for America, Fanny and her school, Tom's illness, even his frustrations over *Hyperion*.

When he left he was carrying a grouse that she had given him for Tom's dinner. They had agreed that he was to come and see her from time to time, but she had cautioned him to be discreet about it for fear of displeasing Mr. O'Callaghan, her "protector."

Keats walked home filled with mixed notions and, typical writer, he did not order or understand his own thoughts until he was back at his writing table, pen in hand. As he set it all down on paper step by step, in a letter to the one person in whom he could most easily confide the incident, his brother George, he rapidly discovered that he had "no libidinous thought about her." He felt a conscious relief in the discovery, for being in love at this point could only increase his difficulties. "I cannot think of those things now Tom is so unwell and weak. Notwithstanding your happiness and your recommendation I hope I shall never marry. Though the most beautiful creature were waiting for me at the end of a journey or a walk; though the carpet were of silk, the curtains of the morning clouds; the chairs and sofa stuffed with cygnet's down; the food manna, the wine beyond claret, the window opening on Winander mere . . . The roaring of the wind is my wife and the stars through the window pane are my children."

What he did not express, even to George, was a secret self-consciousness about his increasing interest in women, not this one or that one, but any one, and his quick physical response to them, his yearnings for "the voice and shape of a woman." He did not want to grow so passionate and susceptible that it might distract him from his writing and study. His concept of beauty was mighty and abstract; he did "not live in this world alone but in a thousand worlds," and his greatest passion was "for the beautiful, connected and made one with the ambition of my intellect."

He was grateful for his emotional freedom; his literary friends understood his isolation; such relationships as theirs could be laid down when necessity demanded and resumed without apology.

On a November afternoon, not long after his letter to George, he walked over to see the Dilkes, taking an unhurried pace to enjoy the brisk air after the stuffy sick room. Leafless branches made black traceries against the gray sky, and the roadside grasses were turning from green to brown, and because these things were all nature-made Keats could enjoy them. He turned down the gently curving lane that led to Wentworth Place, and when the graceful, simple lines of the white stucco house set back from the road in a frame of trees and shrubs came into view it gave him a feeling of peace and well being. He was smiling as he lifted the knocker of the front door. When Mrs. Dilke opened to him, he heard the unfamiliar voices of several persons inside.

"Come in, John; you are in time to meet our visitors."

He was presented first to Mrs. Frances Brawne, the widow who had rented Brown's half of the house last summer when he and Keats were on their walking tour in Scotland, and then to her oldest daughter, Miss Frances Brawne—Fanny.

A pair of remarkably blue eyes that sparkled on the verge of flirting, light brown hair parted in the middle and drawn down on either side of the face in the latest fashion, caught back with blue ribbons the same color as her eyes, a petite and stylishly clad figure—no taller than himself!

Let me begin my dream . . .

"Sit with us a while, Keats," said Dilke. "Brown will probably come in from next door to join us after a bit."

Her profile was better than her full face; she had "a fine style of countenance of the lengthened sort," and she moved with properly trained grace.

A smile of such delight,
As brilliant and as bright . . .

She was cultured, he discovered; she knew music, played

the pianoforte, was proficient in French, liked to dance, loved books and reading. Had he read Mrs. Shelley's new book, *Frankenstein?* she wanted to know. No, but he surely intended to. And did she know Charles Lamb's writings? Yes, indeed; and she enjoyed his droll humor. She had heard that Mr. Keats was a poet, although she had to confess she didn't read much poetry, since she preferred novels. His mother had preferred novels, he told her.

John Keats returned to Tom later than he had intended, and Tom noticed at once his freshly elated state. He'd fallen into some interesting company, John explained—those people who rented Brown's house last summer—the Brawnes.

"Are you excited over a middle-aged widow?" Tom teased, and his brother grinned. No, it was not the widow, but her oldest offspring.

"Describe her to me."

"Oh, she is something of a minx. I think she could be quite fiery if roused."

He busied himself with lighting candles, and when he turned to look at Tom again his brother had dozed off. He had wanted to tell Tom that Fanny was beautiful and that he intended to see her as often as possible.

Later, when Tom awakened, John's attention was entirely diverted into the welfare of his patient, because each time that Tom opened his eyes their gaze seemed farther away, his interest in what went on about him fainter. His face grew more and more gaunt during November as the last remaining flesh melted away from under his skin, and his temperature burned continually high. John sat late by his side at night, half afraid to sleep lest he find his brother gone when he awakened.

Day by day during the latter part of November John felt himself dragged down by continuous loss of sleep. Sometimes he did not lie down himself until nearly morning, dropping off briefly, to start up quickly and discover whether there was still a vestige of vitality in his patient. Tom's mood changed to crossness and excitability and oversensitivity. When John tried to perform a simple bedside service one day, Tom's feelings were suddenly hurt to the point of tears.

John's grief accumulated at the obvious imminence of his brother's end as the disease went into its concluding rapid phase. The sympathetic and devoted Joseph Severn tried to relieve him, but John Keats would have none of it. He must take care of his own brother. It was his family—his own—he was the oldest—their foster father, their minister, their doctor . . .

But was there nothing?

No, nothing that Severn could do.

Tom sank lower, and John scarcely left the room at all. On the night of November 30 he gave no thought to sleep, his doctor's training telling him that this was the last night but one or two. It was the last night. In an early hour of the next day Tom began to choke, suffocate, and with a little rippling sigh he was gone.

John slid the pillows from under Tom's head, straightened his body, closed his eyes, laid his hands gently on his breast, and tiptoed out of the room, down the stairs, and into the roadway. The first tints of morning were beginning to light the sky. He glanced up at the house once, then turned and began to walk toward Wentworth Place. The entrance to Brown's half was around to the left, and Keats stepped silently inside. Finding Brown still asleep he took hold of his hand. Brown started, mumbled, and sat bolt upright when he saw who it was.

"Tom is no more," John whispered and sat beside him on the bed for several moments.

At length Brown spoke, "Have nothing more to do with

those lodgings—and alone too. Had you not better live with me?"

"I think it would be better," John replied, and pressed his friend's hand warmly.

CHAPTER X

Inspect the Lyre

BROWN'S HALF of Wentworth Place consisted of two bedrooms upstairs and two sitting rooms on the ground floor. On either floor the rooms were separated by a narrow hallway and staircase. Keats occupied the back bedroom and the parlor beneath it, where full-length casement windows gave him ready access to the small private garden behind the house. There he sat often, absorbing the secluded peace.

The cloud of grief lifted gradually, a fragment here, another there, and after Keats had been at Wentworth Place for a while he began to move along his old social lifelines again. He went with Brown to the theater to see a new and much discussed play, and another day to Walthamstow to see his sister. He called on Hazlitt and visited Lamb, went to town to dine with Haydon. Bentley the postman came over with a whole clothes basketful of books he had left behind at Well Walk. Joseph Severn showed him the miniature he had done of him; it was to go on exhibition at the Royal Academy.

"Will it not hurt you?" Keats asked naïvely. "What good can it do to any future picture? Even a large picture is lost in that canting place."

Leigh Hunt took Keats and Brown to the Novellos for an evening of music and conversation, and Keats was surprised to find himself bored with the affair. The music was Mozart, and he felt indifferent to it. The humor of the evening consisted largely of time-worn puns, and he was tired of this sort of thing. Most of all he was tired of Leigh Hunt, who now seemed egotistical and lacking in taste. Hunt did one harm by making "fine things petty and beautiful things hateful." It was Hunt's influence, confound it, that had spoiled Mozart for him. Keats came home feeling no inclination ever to meet with any of the group again. The price an artist must pay for his own growth was to outgrow his friends.

But into the void left by the palling of old friendships and the loss of Tom a new love flowed, one that developed and flowered quickly in the hour of need, and John Keats accepted it and turned to it with his whole being. The few hundred paces between Wentworth Place and Elm Cottage where the Brawnes lived grew shorter and shorter, and his visits to Miss Fanny Brawne more and more frequent. He encouraged her to serious reading—poetry, even Hazlitt's lectures—and she banished her younger brother and sister from the parlor when he was there. For him she was serious and then delightfully silly; somber, then coquettish. They had little tiffs and made up quickly, devastated one another with outlandish puns, and carried their merriment to the tea table.

John Keats reveled in the love he had feared and spurned just a few weeks before.

> Cupid, empire-sure,
> Flutter'd and laugh'd, and oft-times through the throng
> Made a delighted way.

Fanny Brawne played the pianoforte for him often. The rhythm of her hands and the tinkling notes lured his tablet out of his pocket, and she watched as he dispelled on paper a late lingering fragment of his grief:

I had a dove and the sweet dove died . . .

Mrs. Brawne had at first encouraged Keats to call on her daughter, but out of the corner of his mind's eye he watched her vacillate between conviction and misgivings. As the whisperings of others reached her ears, she became assailed by doubts. He earned nothing, had little, had given up medical studies, and had a rather ordinary background. The automatic lady in her, though, would not allow her to be openly uncordial, and she invited him to spend Christmas Day with them. Without a moment's hesitation he accepted, although he had promised to join Brown in Chichester for Christmas. Brown had gone down there for the holidays with the additional idea of paying a visit to the home of Dilke's father nearby.

John Keats arrived at Elm Cottage with a firm decision made, his courage screwed to the sticking point, his heart failing him a little when he saw that some of the other guests were hopeful young men seeking out the sparkling Fanny in her becoming new tiny-waisted dress. Ah, how she understood colors and how to select those which suited her best! And the tints and tones in her glorious hair . . .

O latest-born and loveliest vision far . . .

His confidence flooded back when she left her other admirers and greeted him with both hands outstretched. He took a long time kissing them, oblivious to his audience, until he raised his head and saw the gay, smiling group that had closed in around him.

"Splendid, dear fellow!"

"Executed like a true poet!"

She led him into the room by the hand as easily as a lamb is guided by a halter of blossoms, and his genial disposition brought to the gathering the tonic touch it had needed. He was a glamorous figure to the young, who had not learned to worry about the economics of existence; and, while the reviews in the Tory papers had been fierce, they *had* given him considerable space. He really was something of a name in current letters, with the courage to associate himself with a minority.

John Keats, with his reddish-brown hair stylishly long and a bit tousled, his Byronic collar, his expressive and sensitive face, his ebullient gaiety in company, was willing enough to display his histrionic talents in an impersonation or the recitation of one of his own poems. Soon he had to beg for respite. Why? Oh, his throat seemed dry and rough. Well, now, that was quickly repaired with a bit of claret.

He wanted to talk to Fanny alone, but until the volume of Christmas Day callers subsided it wasn't possible. The daylight was fading when he guided her to a window seat, slipping his arm around her waist, and she held his face between her hands and kissed his lips.

> O! save, in charity,
> The quickest pulse for me.

> Save it for me, sweet love! though music breathe
> Voluptuous visions into the warm air . . .

This was his life, his world, his destiny, and he was in love completely. He was her slave, her happy, happy slave, and she must love him in return. She must marry him, she must, she must. . . . With her fingertips she checked the excited flow of words to tell him that she accepted his proposal, that she loved him, and that they were both happy slaves.

O love! how potent hast thou been to teach
Strange journeyings! Wherever beauty dwells,
In gulf or aerie, mountains or deep dells,
In light, in gloom, in star or blazing sun,
Thou pointest out the way, and straight 'tis won.

Floating midway between heaven and earth they took their news to Mrs. Brawne and felt immediately the weight of her conservative view of the match.

"Fanny is only eighteen," she reminded John. "Wait a while. Do not mention your betrothal to too many yet."

In blissful confusion they consented and soon after exchanged engagement rings.

New love, restored spirit, healed grief, retreating fatigue, and John Keats's bright star began to rise above the horizon; a new elation and mounting maturity carried him back to his writing table, and during December 1818 he produced two gay and highly competent poems in trochaic tetrameter rhymed couplets: "To Fancy" and "Bards of Passion."

The first was deeply impulsive, the extroverted expression of an extroverted young man in love for the first time:

Ever let the Fancy roam,
Pleasure never is at home:
At a touch sweet Pleasure melteth
Like to bubbles when rain pelteth;
Then let winged Fancy wander
Through the thought still spread beyond her:
Open wide the mind's cage-door,
She'll dart forth, and cloudward soar.
O sweet Fancy! let her loose;
Summer's joys are spoilt by use,
And the enjoying of the Spring
Fades as does its blossoming . . .

The second, "Bards of Passion," was a better effort, more

precise and careful without losing any of the ardor that had
set it into motion:

> Bards of Passion and of Mirth,
> Ye have left your souls on earth!
> Have ye souls in heaven too,
> Double-lived in regions new?
> Yes, and those of heaven commune
> With the spheres of sun and moon;
> With the noise of fountains wond'rous,
> And the parle of voices thund'rous . . .

Perhaps some of the criticisms of *Endymion* had been de-
served. Perhaps Hunt had influenced his style too much.
Hunt's style was saccharine, filled with Italian influences. He
must forget Hunt. He must write with more vigor, create
images on a grander scale, with less profusion of words, on
big canvases.

His muse and his love were one, not two lures taking him
in different directions as he had feared they might, and out
of this marvelous fusion could come poetry that would sur-
vive long after he himself had left the scene.

"I think I shall be among the English poets after my death,"
he had written to George only recently.

Visions grandiose, yet honest, filled his mind, and his brain
felt keener, clearer, richer, than it ever had before. Oh, he
would write, write, write . . . There must be a poem to Fanny
Brawne, to his love-and-muse-in-one, and to be justly extolled
she could not be confined to the cramping fourteen lines of a
sonnet. The sonnet was too limited a sphere for either of
them. Fanny, to be properly extolled, needed full fifty-six
lines and the self-determining, lilting meters of an ode.

That done, he fingered once more the manuscript of *Hyperion*. Even this poem, so long inhibited, began to move. Ah,
this one was to have muscle, strength. The portrait of the

father of the sun, moon, and dawn must be drawn in bold, heavy strokes. He would benefit by the criticisms of *Endymion*, build upon them, make a poem that they could not call "immature and feverish," the "sickly fancy of a cockney rhymester."

> But one of the whole mammoth-brood still kept
> His sov'reignty, and rule, and majesty;
> Blazing Hyperion on his orbed fire
> Still sat, still snuff'd the incense . . .

Once more Keats entered into mystical communion with the Greek gods and fathers of the gods, but their stride faltered and his faltered with them. What was it that locked a man's mind, that laid a hand over his mental vision when he wanted to create? Maybe his recurring sore throat bothered him more than he realized. Perhaps he ought to join Brown in Chichester where the weather was bound to be milder. Perhaps if he withdrew from familiar things again and withdrew even from his new love and his new happiness, he could complete *Hyperion*.

The compulsion to create was proving too powerful to resist, and the urge to travel in some direction quickly combined with it. Travel released resources within him. In his imagination he lived more out of England than in it: in Latmos, Tartary, the Allegheny Ridge, Savoy.

During the third week of January he took his leave of Fanny and the Dilkes and set out to join Brown. The English landscape that time of year lacked its verdant luster, but it was moving past the coach window, and the hills in the distance never lost their rhythm or their grace.

He arrived in the ancient cathedral town of Chichester in his usual state of exhaustion from the long stage journey, his throat worse, and the solicitous Brown put him to bed.

"Old Mr. Dilke and several other folk are eager to have us

visit them," Brown told him, "but that can wait until you are able."

He recovered quickly, and in a few days he and Brown were able to relive a fragment of their walking tour by covering on foot some thirteen miles along Chichester Harbor to Bedhampton, where Dilke's brother-in-law lived in an old mill house. The day was bright, the countryside secluded, and the high wind on their faces brought back to Keats a memory of his brisk walk along the water's edge in the cheek-burning wind with Isabella. This January wind was sharper and colder than that at Hastings. January . . . Isabella had once told him of an old January legend, the Eve of St. Agnes. Agnes, patron saint of virgins, had died a martyr at the age of thirteen at the beginning of the fourth century, and the legend was that a maiden could hope to dream of her future husband on St. Agnes Eve, January 20, if she went supperless to bed.

John Keats and his friend spent the week end at Bedhampton beside the still and peaceful millpond fringed with trees, and on Monday rode out in a chaise to nearby Stansted to see a new chapel consecrated. Keats's imagination had been dwelling on the St. Agnes story, and witnessing the long religious service brought it into focus. It was not hard to visualize his lovely young heroine, Madeline—not unlike Fanny Brawne—kneeling among the worshipers.

The St. Agnes Eve legend had not suited the worldly Isabella, but it did suit the young and innocent Fanny. Perhaps if she believed in the St. Agnes Eve legend she had gone supperless to bed, lying with eyes closed, awaiting "visions of delight," hoping for soft adorings from him, hoping that he would cross the moors to her, steal into her room, act out her vision . . .

Brown returned to London the day after their visit to the chapel, and Keats remained in Bedhampton to write this sudden poem.

He wrote freely and with spontaneity. Gone was the confusion of too many words; gone were the amateur's artifices
and digressions. A poem flowed from his mind with its expressions clear and its stanzas well disciplined. He had returned almost unconsciously for "The Eve of St. Agnes" to
the Spenserian stanza with its eight lines of iambic pentameter
plus the alexandrine, its rhyme scheme *ababbcbcc*. Yet, for all
its formality, "St. Agnes" was free, rhythmic, melodic; it was
filled with color—purple riot, torch's flame, silver cross, soft
amethyst, silver twilight, cloth of woven crimson, gold and
jet; it had dramatic contrasts—between the noisy festivities
and the quiet retreat of a private chamber, between the youth
of the lovers and the aged, between the cold January night and
the heart on fire.

With Porphyro the poet ventured into the bedchamber of
the young woman they were both in love with:

> Soon, trembling in her soft and chilly nest,
> In sort of wakeful swoon, perplex'd she lay,
> Until the poppied warmth of sleep oppress'd
> Her soothed limbs, and soul fatigued away;
> Flown, like a thought, until the morrow-day;
> Blissfully haven'd both from joy and pain;
> Clasp'd like a missal where swart Paynims pray;
> Blinded alike from sunshine and from rain,
> As though a rose should shut, and be a bud again.

Young Porphyro must wait for his bride, and so must Keats.

> 'Ah, Porphyro!' said she, 'but even now
> 'Thy voice was at sweet tremble in mine ear,
> 'Made tuneable with every sweetest vow;
> 'And those sad eyes were spiritual and clear:
> 'How chang'd thou art! how pallid, chill, and drear!
> 'Give me that voice again, my Porphyro,
> 'Those looks immortal, those complainings dear!
> 'Oh leave me not in this eternal woe,
> 'For if thou diest, my Love, I know not where to go.'

His state of mind profoundly improved, Keats returned to Wentworth Place on the first of February, 1819, and there he was obliged to remain indoors for the better part of two weeks to recover from his exposure to the weather. But he had moved back into a circle of warm indulgence and protection: Brown, Mrs. Dilke, Fanny and Fanny's mother, Severn, and even on occasion the Hunts; and his *Hyperion* manuscript seemed attractive again.

Old problems waited to beset him once more. The ubiquitous Abbey would not allow Fanny Keats to return to her school and was making it increasingly difficult for John to see her. Haydon was around borrowing money, some of it from Keats, his lavishness having caught up with him. All hope of sales for *Endymion* had vanished. There was still no letter from George.

But during the fading winter and approaching spring, Keats spent long, happy—and disturbing—hours with Fanny Brawne. She became his copyist and his encourager, and he did experience productive hours at his writing table. As soon as the weather permitted he sat in the garden behind the house, tablet in hand. And there were greedy enriching hours of reading: Byron, Coleridge, Shelley; and always something to be gleaned by rereading a Shakespeare play.

Clearly and more clearly, in this his twenty-fourth year, John Keats felt the subtleties of his art come under his control and command. Freely and more freely he allowed his imagination to lead him where it would. If a poem he had begun was interrupted by another, he wisely laid the first aside and followed the second. Thus *Hyperion* was crowded into the background in February when he began to write "The Eve of St. Mark" as a companion piece to "St. Agnes." But "St. Mark" after little more than a hundred lines lost its fluency, seemed more jingling than musical, and he turned instead to experimentation with sonnet forms.

Why did I laugh to-night? No voice will tell:
  No God, no Demon of severe response,
Deigns to reply from Heaven or from Hell.
  Then to my human heart I turn at once.
Heart! Thou and I are here sad and alone;
  I say, why did I laugh? O mortal pain!
O Darkness! Darkness! ever must I moan,
  To question Heaven and Hell and Heart in vain.
Why did I laugh? I know this Being's lease,
  My fancy to its utmost blisses spreads;
Yet would I on this very midnight cease,
  And the world's gaudy ensigns see in shreds;
Verse, Fame, and Beauty are intense indeed,
But Death intenser—Death is Life's high meed.

Its rhyme scheme was Shakespearean, and so were "On a Dream" and "Bright Star," and in them he had broken away from the Italian influence for good. But even the Shakespearean sonnet did not satisfy him now. It was another poet's achievement, not his; and he must create his own. He must take all that he knew, everything that the poets of mankind had learned so far, and add something more, something fresh, something that would live longer than himself. This was the artist's ultimate search.

"Brown and I sit opposite one another all day authorizing," he wrote in one of his cumulative letters to George. "He is at present writing a story of an old woman who lived in a forest . . . On Monday we had to dinner Severn and Cawthorn the bookseller and print virtuoso . . . we are to have a party this evening . . . a few days ago Hunt dined here . . . another satire is expected from Byron called *Don Giovanni* [*Don Juan*] . . . I was surprised to hear from Taylor the amount of Murray the Booksellers last sale—what do you think of £25,000? He sold 4,000 copies of Lord Byron . . ."

In that same letter, begun the middle of February and concluded the end of April, he told his brother of meeting Coleridge on a walk toward Highgate. Coleridge was with his literary executor, Joseph Henry Green, whom Keats recognized as a former staff assistant at Guy's Hospital. The three paced along together for two miles, and Keats found the senior poet more garrulous than himself; for once in his life Keats was out-talked.

"In those two miles he broached a thousand things—let me see if I can give you a list—nightingales, poetry—on poetical sensation—metaphysics—different genera and species of dreams —nightmare—a dream accompanied with a sense of touch—single and double touch—a dream related—first and second consciousness—the difference explained between will and volition—so many metaphysicians from a want of smoking—the second consciousness—monsters—the Kraken—mermaids —Southey believes in them—Southey's belief too much diluted—a ghost story—good morning. I heard his voice as he came towards me. I heard it as he moved away. I had heard it all the interval."

As they parted company the two poets clasped hands, and Keats did not understand the expression of sudden surprise in Coleridge's face. He did not know that Coleridge found his hand hot—much too hot—and too damp. All Keats understood about himself then was that he burned with the fervor and brilliance of creativity—and longing—spiritual longing for that poem more brilliant and clear than "St. Agnes" and physical longing for his promised bride.

During the early part of April his pen was almost mute because his bride drew closer to him and at the same time remained unattainable. It was a deeply disturbing time, when the indulgent and attentive Dilkes moved from Wentworth Place to London, and Mrs. Brawne and her three children leased their half of the house. Fanny was now right next door, within reach of his hand had there been no partition, sleeping so very near him at night!

Both Brown and Reynolds were frank about their disapproval of the arrangement, and did not pretend to understand Mrs. Brawne's motives or lack of discernment, because John Keats was incapable of concealing his infatuation. During 1819 Charles Armitage Brown was closest to Keats of all his friends, and he gave Keats more care than Keats was aware of, administering the household, watching his health when his sore throat recurred, rescuing discarded scraps of paper that contained verses. Carefully he helped Keats recover his equilibrium, lured him back to their daily writing routine. Good old Brown! Brown's lips tightened when he saw John and Fanny sharing the same garden, or watched his poet-friend look up from his work with a confused start at the sound of Fanny's footstep or the tinkle of her pianoforte on the other side of the wall.

But Keats's muse was his first mistress, and gradually his stability returned and he dabbled a bit in some Spenserian stanzas "On Charles Armitage Brown," taking them next door—how convenient, really!—for Fanny to copy. Fanny, he could see, was falling deeper and deeper into love with him, but—innocent and unawakened and not fully understanding—she was carelessly provocative at times and sent him back to his own quarters in a state of unbearable elation, bursting with frustrated desire. At such times there could be no sleep, and he lit a candle and sat down before sheets of paper, pen in hand.

> O what can ail thee, knight-at-arms,
>   Alone and palely loitering?
> The sedge has wither'd from the lake,
>   And no birds sing.

. . .
I saw pale kings and princes too,
 Pale warriors, death-pale were they all;
They cried—'La Belle Dame sans Merci
 Hath thee in thrall!'

I saw their starved lips in the gloam,
 With horrid warning gaped wide,
And I awoke and found me here,
 On the cold hill's side.

And this is why I sojourn here,
 Alone and palely loitering,
Though the sedge is wither'd from the lake,
 And no birds sing.

Here was a further ascendency in his art, and he was acutely aware of it. Never before had he said so much with so few words, nor resolved a theme richer in symbolism, nor struck a clearer melody. The ballad, "La Belle Dame sans Merci," had the twang of the lyre in it. With utmost honesty and boyish candor he hurried to his beloved copyist next day with the ballad in his hand.

His *Hyperion* manuscript, left abruptly in the middle of Book III at the word "celestial," lost its importance in the light of his new lyrical mood, and he decided to abandon it; it was not really so original as he had supposed. It was too Miltonic, too similar in style to *Paradise Lost*. His mind suddenly freed of the project, he plunged wholeheartedly into capturing the melodies ringing in his ears.

First came "Song of Four Fairies" that begins with the rhythm borrowed so obviously from "Double, double, toil and trouble," reversed into "Happy, happy glowing fire," a fruit of the poet's ardent zest, far more of a bridge between great poems than one itself. After a superb result like "La Belle Dame" there was bound to be a temporary flagging.

Next he produced the sonnets, "To Sleep" and "On Fame,"
and in them he had recovered his level and was soaring again.

To Cupid, "empire-sure," he turned once more, identifying
himself with the Greek god of love, in love himself with the
mortal and supremely beautiful Psyche, who achieved immortality by her marriage to Cupid.

> O Goddess! hear these tuneless numbers, wrung
>   By sweet enforcement and remembrance dear,
> And pardon that thy secrets should be sung
>   Even into thine own soft-conched ear:
> Surely I dreamt to-day, or did I see
>   The winged Psyche with awaken'd eyes?
> I wander'd in a forest thoughtlessly,
>   And, on the sudden, fainting with surprise,
> Saw two fair creatures, couched side by side . . .

He could not be sure any more how much of his time
spent with Fanny was real and how much was dream. Where
did one end and the other begin?

> They lay calm-breathing on the bedded grass;
>   Their arms embraced, and their pinions too;
>   Their lips touch'd not, but had not bade adieu . . .

Oh, our lips have touched, beloved Fanny, and have not
bade adieu, but I still do not have

> Thy shrine, thy grove, thy oracle, thy heat
>   Of pale-mouth'd prophet dreaming.

> Yes, I will be thy priest, and build a fane
>   In some untrodden region of my mind,
> Where branched thoughts, new grown with pleasant pain,
>   Instead of pines shall murmur in the wind:

> . . .

> And in the midst of this wide quietness
> A rosy sanctuary will I dress

With the wreath'd trellis of a working brain,
    With buds, and bells, and stars without a name,
With all the gardener Fancy e'er could feign,
    Who breeding flowers, will never breed the same:
And there shall be for thee all soft delight
    That shadowy thought can win,
A bright torch, and a casement ope at night,
    To let the warm Love in!

"Ode to Psyche" was the first of his five most important odes, all written during April and May of 1819.

He had taken "moderate pains" with it, he told George. For the most part his poems were "dashed off," but this one he had done leisurely and carefully. "I think it reads more richly for it."

He reread his "latest-born and loveliest vision far" and experienced a deep thrill. His mind had never been so awake or so facile. It had never been so sensitive. These days, any slight stimulation—a compliment, a note of music, a kiss, a brief legend—unleashed an abundance of poetic matter with all its moods, pictures, phrases, words, tears, laughter, colors, sounds.

He took "Psyche" to Fanny and glanced up now and again at her face as he read it to her, wondering whether she was in love with him or his poetry.

"Read me the part again beginning, 'Yes, I will be thy priest . . .'"

He complied, and with supreme gentleness she gathered the sheets of paper from his hands so that she could make a perfect copy of the poem.

"Fanny, dearest love! Sweet home of all my fears, and hopes and joys, and miseries. . . !"

Her face filled with compassion at the line from her own ode, and she slipped her arms around his neck, pressed her lips into his ear, "Dearest!"

"Fanny! We must *marry!*"

"Mamma won't permit it yet. We must wait . . ."

"I can't remain here so close to you and wait. Are you content to wait?"

"Yes," she whispered. "I am content to wait a while."

Petulantly he toyed and plucked at the sleeve of her dress, a puffing thing she had designed herself, and pleaded, "Sit in the garden with me this evening."

"Mamma and I are going to the military dance tonight."

A sudden rush of angry jealousy stained his face, and he fairly choked, "You are betrothed to me!"

"Dearest, dearest John! I am betrothed to you, and I love you. But I do not want to give up my social life until we are wed, and Mama doesn't want me to."

He took her arms from around his neck and held the hands that could play, design, sew, and write in a clear sweeping script.

"I know," he said, studying the tips of her fingers, "that I must do something decisive. I must resolve to earn a living. Perhaps I can go back to medicine."

She tugged at him to get him to his feet. "Darling," she said, "Mama wants us to come to tea."

The moody moment was dispelled slowly at table, and after tea Keats went disconsolately out of the front door and around to his own quarters.

Perhaps he ought to learn some of the newest dance steps that she liked so well; perhaps he ought to live farther away from her. The real solution would be to write something that would sell like *Childe Harold*.

How much of *Endymion* had been prescience? Was his own love a Greek goddess, holding court, withholding herself, casting spells? Would she leave him at last upon some ancient mountainside and "medicine death into a lengthen'd drowsiness?"

Seeking release in his work, and within his work seeking escape into the cool, pure realms of the mind, to be freed of the heat and pain of mortal love for a brief moment, he dwelt upon the lore of Greece and Attic loveliness. The marble purity of Grecian beauty—its truth. What the imagination seizes as beauty must be truth.

John Keats's "Ode on a Grecian Urn" was both inevitable and incredible. It was inevitable that he should by now have struggled free of the sonnet with its fourteen-line prejudice to create this ten-line stanza and its two pairs of lines and two sets of triple rhymes, inevitable that in developing his own style he should have resorted, like so many romantic poets, to the flexible ancient choral form, in the manner of Horace, inevitable even that he should have resolved his philosophic search at this his period of most superb creativity. And yet, "Ode on a Grecian Urn" is incredible in its approach to poetic perfection. Its beauty is both intellectual and spiritual. In its writing John Keats achieved a dissociation from the sensual cares that bedeviled him, lifted himself from the dark and confused mountain paths and darkling forests and flew through the air, earth free.

> Thou still unravish'd bride of quietness,
>   Thou foster-child of silence and slow time,
> Sylvan historian, who canst thus express
>   A flowery tale more sweetly than our rhyme:
> What leaf-fring'd legend haunts about thy shape
>   Of deities or mortals, or of both,
>   In Tempe or the dales of Arcady?
> What men or gods are these? What maidens loth?
> What mad pursuit? What struggle to escape?
>   What pipes and timbrels? What wild ecstasy?
>
> Heard melodies are sweet, but those unheard
>   Are sweeter; therefore, ye soft pipes, play on;

Not to the sensual ear, but, more endear'd,
  Pipe to the spirit ditties of no tone:
Fair youth, beneath the trees, thou canst not leave
    Thy song, nor ever can those trees be bare;
    Bold Lover, never, never canst thou kiss,
Though winning near the goal—yet, do not grieve;
    She cannot fade, though thou hast not thy bliss,
      For ever wilt thou love, and she be fair!

Ah, happy, happy boughs! that cannot shed
  Your leaves, nor ever bid the Spring adieu;
And, happy melodist, unwearied,
  For ever piping songs for ever new;
More happy love! more happy, happy love!
  For ever warm and still to be enjoy'd,
    For ever panting and for ever young;
All breathing human passion far above,
    That leaves a heart high-sorrowful and cloy'd
      A burning forehead, and a parching tongue.

Who are these coming to the sacrifice?
  To what green altar, O mysterious priest,
Lead'st thou that heifer lowing at the skies,
  And all her silken flanks with garlands drest?
What little town by river or sea shore,
  Or mountain-built with peaceful citadel,
    Is emptied of this folk, this pious morn?
And, little town, thy streets for evermore
  Will silent be; and not a soul to tell
    Why thou art desolate, can e'er return.

O Attic shape! Fair attitude! with brede
  Of marble men and maidens overwrought,
With forest branches and the trodden weed;
  Thou, silent form, dost tease us out of thought
As doth eternity: Cold Pastoral!
  When old age shall this generation waste,
    Thou shalt remain, in midst of other woe

> Than ours, a friend to man, to whom thou say'st,
>   Beauty is truth, truth beauty,—that is all
>   Ye know on earth, and all ye need to know

The almost surrealist level attained during the hours of pure creativity began to recede from him, and he had to find his way back to everyday affairs. Returning was a downward journey, like the descent into sleep, except that this descent was toward melancholy. He tried the disciplines of reading, walking, the forced gaiety of social gatherings. But the melancholy fit was falling about him "from heaven like a weeping cloud." At length he surrendered himself up to it and wrote his "Ode on Melancholy."

> She dwells with Beauty—Beauty that must die;
>   And Joy, whose hand is ever at his lips
> Bidding adieu; and aching Pleasure nigh,
>   Turning to poison while the bee-mouth sips:
> Ay, in the very temple of Delight
>   Veil'd Melancholy has her sovran shrine,
>   Though seen of none save him whose strenuous tongue
> Can burst Joy's grape against his palate fine;
>   His soul shall taste the sadness of her might,
>   And be among her cloudy trophies hung.

A long letter full of good news from George in America aided the rebuilding of his morale, and he wrote a short note to his sister promising to walk over to Walthamstow with it within the next few days. "They are quite well and settled tolerably in comfort after a great deal of fatigue and harass," he assured Fanny Keats.

He had more to tell her when he saw her, because he was beginning on another fit of resolve to find some way to earn a living so that he and Fanny Brawne could be married. He was going to take a voyage or two aboard a ship plying between England and India as ship's doctor. He had even begun to sort out his effects, discard worthless notes, burn letters, return borrowed books.

But why did these tasks weary him so quickly? Perhaps because he really did not want to change his pattern of living or give up his "fevrous life alone with poetry."

He sank onto a chair in his back parlor, close to the floor-length windows that were standing ajar to the mild late spring evening, and pulled another chair to him so that he could lean his elbow on its back. The song of a nightingale very nearby filled the garden and the room, and under its influence John Keats's muse crept back to his side.

The nightingale that he heard was one of a pair that had built their nest in the garden only this spring. The fragile nest, fashioned of leaves and roots in the shape of a deep cup, lined with soft fibers and feathers, hidden in the grass and undergrowth of the Wentworth Place garden, already contained its five or six olive-green eggs, and he and Brown and the Brawnes watched the progress of the family discreetly lest they frighten them off. They might never have noticed the little dull reddish-brown bird but for his marvelous song.

As Keats listened to the varying, plaintive, rich tones, he lost track of how long he sat by the garden window, but the nightingale's spell lasted on through the evening, even when Joseph Severn appeared with some others and took him off to a local tavern.

Severn was feeling at his expansive best these days, because of the recognition his pictures were receiving, and as he and Keats and several others sat about the inn table, laughing and joking, Severn began to hold forth on a fine point of art. The inn windows were open to the warm night air, and the scent of nearby pines drifted in. A sound outside caused Keats to lose all interest in the conversation, and he slipped away and out-of-doors, to the grove of pine trees, there to seat himself upon a low escarpment of ground to listen to the song of a nightingale. He listened to the music from the bursting little throat, until he became aware of Severn standing a few feet away. The painter, not knowing what was wrong, had come to seek him.

Next morning at breakfast Keats was almost completely silent, and Brown did not break in upon his revery. Scarcely had they finished eating than Keats took his chair out to the garden and sat under a plum tree, long thin sheets of paper in hand. He remained in the garden almost the entire morning, struggling with phrases: "light-winged Dryad of the trees . . . singest of summer in full-throated ease . . . thou hast never known the weariness, the fever, and the fret . . . the coming musk-rose . . . now more than ever seems it rich to die, to cease upon the midnight with no pain, while thou art pouring forth thy soul abroad in such an ecstacy . . ."

He returned to the house at last and, on seeing Brown, experienced a little twinge of furtiveness and stuffed two sheets filled with writing behind some books on a shelf. Brown reached for the crumpled sheets and looked at them.

"Come," he said. "Show me which of these is first."

Keats arranged the pages one on top of the other and Brown found himself reading his "Ode to a Nightingale."

"Keats," he pleaded, "let me copy this for you, and let me do your copying in the future. Let me see all the bits and pieces that are about the house."

Like an agreeable small boy, Keats consented.

Brown sat down at once and began to transcribe the superbly lovely poem:

My heart aches, and a drowsy numbness pains
    My sense, as though of hemlock I had drunk,
Or emptied some dull opiate to the drains
    One minute past, and Lethe-wards had sunk:
'Tis not through envy of thy happy lot,
    But being too happy in thy happiness,—

That thou, light-winged Dryad of the trees,
  In some melodious plot
Of beechen green, and shadows numberless,
  Singest of summer in full-throated ease.

O, for a draught of vintage! that hath been
  Cool'd a long age in the deep-delved earth,
Tasting of Flora and the country green,
  Dance, and Provençal song, and sunburnt mirth!
O for a beaker full of the warm South,
  Full of the true, the blushful Hippocrene,
    With beaded bubbles winking at the brim,
      And purple-stained mouth;
  That I might drink, and leave the world unseen,
    And with thee fade away into the forest dim:

Fade far away, dissolve, and quite forget
  What thou among the leaves hast never known,
The weariness, the fever, and the fret
  Here, where men sit and hear each other groan;
Where palsy shakes a few, sad, last gray hairs,
  Where youth grows pale, and spectre-thin, and dies;
    Where but to think is to be full of sorrow
      And leaden-eyed despairs,
  Where Beauty cannot keep her lustrous eyes,
    Or new Love pine at them beyond to-morrow.

Away! away! for I will fly to thee,
  Not charioted by Bacchus and his pards,
But on the viewless wings of Poesy,
  Though the dull brain perplexes and retards:
Already with thee! tender is the night,
  And haply the Queen-Moon is on her throne,
    Cluster'd around by all her starry Fays;
      But here there is no light,
  Save what from heaven is with the breezes blown
    Through verdurous glooms and winding mossy ways.

I cannot see what flowers are at my feet,
  Nor what soft incense hangs upon the boughs,
But, in embalmed darkness, guess each sweet
  Wherewith the seasonable month endows
The grass, the thicket, and the fruit-tree wild;
  White hawthorn, and the pastoral eglantine;
    Fast fading violets cover'd up in leaves;
      And mid-May's eldest child,
  The coming musk-rose, full of dewy wine,
    The murmurous haunt of flies on summer eves.

Darkling I listen; and, for many a time
  I have been half in love with easeful Death,
Call'd him soft names in many a mused rhyme,
  To take into the air my quiet breath;
Now more than ever seems it rich to die,
  To cease upon the midnight with no pain,
    While thou art pouring forth thy soul abroad
      In such an ecstasy!
  Still wouldst thou sing, and I have ears in vain—
    To thy high requiem become a sod.

Thou wast not born for death, immortal Bird!
  No hungry generations tread thee down;
The voice I hear this passing night was heard
  In ancient days by emperor and clown:
Perhaps the self-same song that found a path
  Through the sad heart of Ruth, when, sick for home,
    She stood in tears amid the alien corn;
      The same that oft-times hath
  Charm'd magic casements, opening on the foam
    Of perilous seas, in faery lands forlorn.

Forlorn! the very word is like a bell
  To toll me back from thee to my sole self!
Adieu! the fancy cannot cheat so well
  As she is fam'd to do, deceiving elf.

Adieu! adieu! thy plaintive anthem fades
Past the near meadows, over the still stream,
Up the hill-side; and now 'tis buried deep
In the next valley-glades:
Was it a vision, or a waking dream?
Fled is that music:—Do I wake or sleep?

John Keats was a lyricist. His greatest poems are his odes, and the greatest of these is "Ode to a Nightingale."

CHAPTER XI

I Am But a Voice

THE DEEPEST, richest, and best of Keats is in the musical, warm, and voluptuous "Ode to a Nightingale." Keats's heart had ached for a long time; weariness and fever were taxing him heavily; but in the mild evening air and the peace of a garden a sequence of melodic phrases had brought his most compelling passion into its full expression.

A languor followed. "The blissful cloud of summer-indolence benumb'd" his eyes. His pulse "grew less and less; pain had no sting." This new mood creeping upon him was a shadowy experience, something "hushed and muffled," and the images that he saw were "masque-like figures on the dreamy urn." He captured them in his "Ode on Indolence."

But the writing of the ode did not dispell his slowly growing lassitude, and he was finding it increasingly difficult to resolve plans or follow through on programs. By the time the warm June weather reached Hampstead he had given up the idea of being a ship's doctor, because he felt too fatigued to attempt it. His throat was bothering him again, and Brown began to persuade him gently to plan on spending the summer away from Wentworth Place—and away from the Brawnes.

The idea of a cheap lodging in a seashore place did appeal to Keats, and he chatted with this friend and that about possible sites. But when he went up to London to ask Abbey for the necessary cash, Abbey gave him the shocking news that an aunt, the wife of a Jennings uncle, was filing a claim in Chancery against the estate. It meant that the bulk of the estate would be frozen until the slow, toilsome case was settled. John Keats was without any income at all.

Only two days before he had been unable to visit his sister in Walthamstow because of lack of silver, and he had not felt physically able to walk the distance. Now, he remembered the thirty pounds he had loaned Haydon a while ago, and he wrote asking for repayment. The reply that came back—from his friend of such long standing—was a hostile refusal. Haydon simply did not have thirty pounds, and could not see his way clear to worrying about it. He owed much more to others. As soon as his Jerusalem picture was completed and placed on exhibition, he would be able to honor debts and plenty to spare.

To point up Keats's acutely embarrassing financial position still further, an old friend dropped in to ask him to go to Isle of Wight. It was James Rice, the attorney whom he had met through Bailey and the Reynoldses. He was fond of Rice; a month with him on Wight—Rice mentioned Shanklin —would be most pleasant. Rice was ill, needed the rest, and particularly wanted Keats's companionship.

Charles Armitage Brown, ever eager to rescue his friend from both his financial and amorous predicaments, came forward with the money.

"Do go, Keats. You liked Shanklin when you saw it before. We can settle up when your Chancery case is over."

Keats's own native wisdom had been at work; so had his natural instinct of self-preservation. If he were not so near to the woman he loved, perhaps the daylight hours at least would be less distressing; "for at night, when the lonely day has closed, and the lonely, silent, unmusical chamber is waiting to receive me as into a sepulchre, then believe me my passion gets entirely the sway," then his thoughts created strange rhapsodies that must be kept a secret because they proved him either "too unhappy or perhaps a little mad."

Lying in the dark, sleepless, candle extinguished, he did not need to close his eyes to dream of wandering "bent warm on amorous theft" and finding

> A nymph, to whom all hoofed Satyrs knelt;
> At whose white feet the languid Tritons poured
> Pearls . . .

Nymphs, dryads, fauns, satyrs, called up one another and one another's legends, and soon in the "taller grasses and full-flowering weed" he came upon the lagorous, coiling figure of a "palpitating snake." Lamia! the beautiful woman-bugbear, terror of all children, bitter, jealous, now assuming this insidious form, begging to be turned back into the form of a woman.

The story had developed quickly in his mind, and he had begun to write another narrative poem: *Lamia*.

> She was a gordian shape of dazzling hue,
> Vermilion-spotted, golden, green, and blue;
> Striped like a zebra, freckled like a pard,
> Eyed like a peacock, and all crimson barr'd;
> And full of silver moons, that, as she breathed,
> Dissolv'd, or brighter shone, or interwreathed
> Their lustres with the gloomier tapestries . . .
>
>   . . .
>
> Her head was serpent, but ah, bitter-sweet!
> She had a woman's mouth with all its pearls complete . . .

But his nightly phantoms were as provocative and elusive as his real love, and daylight dissolved them before he could record their colors and forms.

When he was packing to set out for Shanklin with Rice, he put the fragment of *Lamia* among his things. Perhaps he could recapture the inspiration while he was away.

As he went around to the front door of Wentworth Place to take farewell of Fanny Brawne, a question lurked deep in his mind: ought he to return to her at all? Ought he not to set her free, even though there could be no freedom for himself from this enslaving love?

This beautiful girl whom he loved . . . here she was to admit him . . . her eyes were brimming over . . . He hurt both of them by staying, both of them by going away.

He had meant to make this farewell brief, but she clung to him and begged him to visit a while, insisted on playing for him on the pianoforte. Did she sense that he thought of not returning? His unhappiness and physical lassitude made him feel old and made her seem very, very young.

"I will write to you," he promised.

"Long, long letters! My beloved, my poet!"

"Long, long letters, my dearest lady."

He got off at last, and he and Rice hurried up to London to catch the south-bound stage.

They rode on top of the coach—with the inevitable result. They traveled through some bad weather and both were soaked through with beating rain and chilled to the bone. Keats's throat grew worse once more, and he and Rice both contracted head colds that required several days of mild weather and sea air to clear up. Keats developed a racking cough that shattered his efforts to concentrate or sleep until at last it subsided into an infrequent hack, although it did not disappear.

Shanklin was as he remembered it from his brief earlier

visit: "sloping wood and meadow . . . cliffs . . . primroses . . .
fishermen's huts . . . steps down to the sand." In his room in
Eglantine Cottage, where they were staying, Keats's writing
table was at a window that looked "over house tops and cliffs
onto the sea, so that when the ships sail past the cottage chim-
neys you may take them for weathercocks. We have hill and
dale, forest and mead, and plenty of lobsters." He had a
little "coffin of a room" but what did that matter if he could
sit at a window overlooking the sea to write.

The first letter that John Keats wrote to Fanny Brawne
from Shanklin he did not send, because it had been written
during those hours when he was either "too unhappy or perhaps a little mad," and in the clear broad light of morning he
destroyed it and began another in a more wholesome tone to
"My dearest lady"—"I am now at a very pleasant cottage
window, looking onto a beautiful hilly country, with a
glimpse of the sea . . . I have never known any unalloy'd
happiness for many days together: the death or sickness of
someone has always spoilt my hours—and now when none
such troubles oppress me, it is you must confess very hard that
another sort of pain should haunt me. Ask yourself, my love,
whether you are not very cruel to have so entrammelled me,
so destroyed my freedom. Will you confess this in the letter
you must write immediately and do all you can to console me
in it . . . Write the softest words and kiss them that I may at
least touch my lips where yours have been."

Next a long newsy letter went to his sister on the sixth of
July, and on the eighth another love letter to Fanny Brawne:
"My sweet girl, your letter gave me more delight than anything in the world but yourself could do; indeed I am almost
astonished that any absent one should have that luxurious
power over my senses which I feel . . . I am miserable that
you are not with me . . . I never knew before, what such a

love as you have made me feel, was; I did not believe in it;
my fancy was afraid of it, lest it should burn me up . . ."

Fanny's letters were as vexatious as her personality at times.
She only half understood this extraordinary kind of love a
poet was bestowing upon her, and she felt some doubts as to
whether it was herself or her beauty he loved.

"Why may I not speak of your beauty, since without that I
could never have lov'd you. I cannot conceive any beginning
of such love as I have for you but beauty. There may be a
sort of love for which, without the least sneer at it, I have
the highest respect, and can admire it in others; but it has not
the richness, the bloom, the full form, the enchantment of
love after my own heart. So let me speak of your beauty . . ."

She needled him with another doubt, her fear that he might
not realize that she really loved him.

"You say you are afraid I shall think you do not love me.
In saying this you make me ache the more to be near you.
. . . I kiss'd your writing over in the hope you had indulg'd
me by leaving a trace of honey . . ."

Many days passed before he could write to her again. He
was in "so irritable a state of health" that he could not write.
He wasn't really *so* ill, he protested to himself; it was just
that he felt teasing and unpleasant. At that point Rice was a
sicker man than Keats, and the two irritated each other to
such a degree that they went on solitary walks and avoided
long conversations for fear of the inevitable quarrel that would
follow. Keats had been mistaken when he wrote to Fanny
Brawne that his hours were not now spoiled by someone's
illness.

"My love, my sweet physician," he wrote to her. "Do
not call it folly, when I tell you I took your letter last night
to bed with me. In the morning I found your name on the
sealing wax obliterated. I was startled at the bad omen." He
filled his missive with chitchat of his efforts to write and

study. "You must write to me—as I will every week—for your letters keep me alive. My sweet girl I cannot speak my love for you. Good night."

Absence was no solution. True, distance from Fanny meant that he could accomplish a little more work, but it could not cure his love.

His letters to his sweetheart, his sister, the Reynoldses, Brown, and others told them more than he realized, and before the end of July Brown was on a coach bound for the southern coast of England to take a boat out to the Isle of Wight and join Keats and Rice. Brown's arrival had a wholesome effect. He'd been there only a few days when Rice decided to move on and spend the rest of his holiday with another companion, and Brown and Keats were left alone. They got on well, these two, because they were accustomed to living together, and because Brown was blessed by good health and a calm disposition.

Brown found Keats in a state of feverish activity, accomplishing little, but studying Greek and Latin, making scattered efforts at writing, a few lines of verse here and there, a little added to *Lamia*. Brown brought all the scattered activity into focus with an idea of his own.

He had a big idea, he told Keats. He hoped that he and Keats could collaborate in writing a play in verse based on the story of Otto I, Emperor of Germany in the tenth century. Keats's first impulse was to laugh at the idea, because he really thought Brown was joking. But the romance and martial vigor of the story soon took hold of his imagination, and he and Brown sat down opposite each other at the same table—as they were used to doing at Wentworth Place—and began to work. Brown happily described characters, action, story structure of each scene as it came along, and Keats wrote dialogue in iambic pentameter.

Charles Armitage Brown knew important people at Drury

Lane Theatre in London; he'd had a play of his own produced there a few years back. With his connections and experience and Keats's writing, their hopes rose from day to day and from scene to scene that they were producing a money-maker.

Good old Brown!

"I am not idle enough for proper down-right love letters," Keats wrote to Fanny Brawne on the fifth of August. "I leave this minute a scene in our tragedy and see you (think it not blasphemy) through the mist of plots, speeches, counterplots and counter speeches. The lover is madder than I am. I am nothing to him. He has a figure like the statue of Meleager and double distilled fire in his heart. Thank God for my diligence! Were it not for that I should be miserable. . ."

He and Brown worked diligently at Shanklin until the middle of August, and for Keats the stimulation of producing multiplied itself. He completed half of *Lamia* and began to work on a new approach to *Hyperion,* reconceiving the whole thing and beginning afresh as *The Fall of Hyperion.*

Brown was in marvelous good spirits, and Keats found him contagious. Really, together they could make a mint with what they were producing. Four acts of *Otho the Great* were completed, and there was only one more act to go. Why did they not go back to the mainland and find a cheaper place to live in the city of Winchester, Brown suggested. They could make this highly productive vacation last longer that way. Keats consented at once. Brown, after all, was not a rich man, and they were both living on his money.

Winchester was large, "an exceeding pleasant town, enriched with a beautiful cathedral and surrounded by a fresh-looking country," Keats wrote to Benjamin Bailey. "We are in tolerably good and cheap lodgings. Within these two months I have written 1500 lines . . ."

There were long walks between columns of tall elm trees.

The whole town was wooded. Outside of town there were clear streams full of trout.

Shortly after they settled in Winchester they began the last act of *Otho,* but when Brown outlined the act to Keats the poet declared it too melodramatic, too filled with a multitude of incidents. Brown let him go ahead and let him write it to suit himself, and when he read the finished manuscript he had but one word to utter, "Enchanting!" Keats grinned. He felt good, lifted above his fatigue, and even his unrequited love, momentarily. Perhaps playwriting was the answer.

"I shall make you popular in spite of your detractors," Brown declared, for they had decided to leave Keats's name off the manuscript when they presented it to the producers. What a great joke on the critics—after they had clapped their hands red—to discover that John Keats had written the play.

"I should like," said Keats, leaning back in his chair and stretching his legs out before him, "to make a great revolution in modern dramatic writing . . . and to upset the drawling of the blue stocking literary world! If in the course of another few years I do these two things I ought to die content—and my friends should drink a dozen of claret on my tomb."

Brown applauded the funeral service.

"A fine writer," Keats went on to philosophize, "is the most genuine being in the world . . . I look upon fine phrases like a lover."

Brown began to talk to Keats about another idea for a play. Had he, Brown queried, ever read the story of Stephen, King of England in the twelfth century, his struggle to keep his crown, and his ultimate defeat? They thought out loud about it together for a while.

"The play must open," said Brown, "with the field of battle, when Stephen's forces are retreating . . ."

"Stop!" said Keats. "Stop! I have been already too long in leading-strings. I will do all this myself."

He set to work at once, with amazing gusto, writing at white heat, when exhaustion and inertia swept over him, and the false energy that had carried him through to the completion of *Otho* was expended. He threw himself upon the bed, flat on his back, eyes closed, arms and legs outstretched, unable to move or think, and not even the first act of *King Stephen* was ever completed.

Slowly he recovered his mobility—went on bracing walks, dined, rested—and when he was able to return to his writing he decided to work on *Lamia*, striving toward its conclusion when the serpent-bride should destroy the bridegroom.

The specter of money—or the lack thereof—had begun to stalk them, and by the end of August Keats and Brown were approaching their last few shillings. Keats wrote to his publishers, Taylor and Hessey; Brown wrote to a friend in Hampshire; each source sent a loan of thirty pounds. In his long letter of appreciation to his publisher, Keats copied in a section from *Lamia*, told them of *Otho*, and explained that he was engaged also on some final revisions of "The Eve of St. Agnes." When he returned to London, his publishers would see that he was still a producing author, that their thirty pounds was really an advance against future work.

He dashed to London sooner than he had thought he would —only five days after writing to Taylor and Hessey—called up by an alarming letter from George Keats. George needed money—suddenly—desperately. In that far-off wilderness George had met the naturalist John James Audubon, who had presented himself as a man of means and talked the twenty-two-year-old George into investing his resources in a commercial riverboat. The boat had scarcely begun carrying its passengers and freight on the Mississippi and Ohio rivers when it foundered and sank. George had lost everything, and he wrote frantically to that ever-protecting older brother. The plea sent John rushing to Abbey, who assured him that he was doing all he could to bring the Jennings lawsuit to a conclusion. As soon as the estate was released, George Keats would receive funds from him, and for that natter so would John.

On his second day in London Keats hurried to the offices of Taylor and Hessey where he found Richard Woodhouse. Eagerly he showed Woodhouse his manuscripts of "St. Agnes" and the now completed *Lamia*. Could they be published right away?

"I liked 'Isabella,' " said Woodhouse.

"That poem seems mawkish to me now," Keats replied.

Woodhouse felt that "Isabella" would have a better chance with the public than "St. Agnes." The latter was rather immoral in spots, and it might fall into the hands of lady readers.

"I do not want ladies to read my poetry," said Keats. "I write for men."

It was Saturday; Woodhouse was pressed by other appointments and planning to leave town on a holiday tomorrow afternoon. And so he invited Keats to have breakfast with him next morning. They could talk until his coach time, he suggested, and Keats concurred.

Over breakfast on Sunday morning Keats discoursed at great length on "St. Agnes," and that done read the entire *Lamia* to Woodhouse. Their tête-à-tête lasted for six hours. Woodhouse believed in Keats; it was his influence that had helped persuade Taylor and Hessey to lend him the thirty pounds so very recently.

"I shall write Taylor an account of our talk," he promised when he and Keats took leave of one another, and Keats knew that he would.

Hopefully Keats returned to Winchester, there to complete

a long, long letter to George and Georgiana, telling them of his conference with Abbey, Abbey's promise of diligence, and including every bit of news he could think of to comfort and divert the worried young couple. He was "reading, writing, and fretting." While up in London he had gone to Walthamstow to see Fanny, and their sister "looked better than I had seen her for some time." Most of their acquaintances were still away in the country and he had not seen them. He went into detail about the play he had written with Brown, about *Lamia*, copied into the letter some of his verses, remembered some additional details of his Scottish trip. He told them of his reading of Dante, his studying of Greek, and toward the end of the long missive reiterated passionately that he would do all he could to send them some money and encourage Abbey to do so.

He had returned to Winchester the middle of September, and it seemed quite chilly. He longed for a fire in his room to mitigate the autumn air which was persistently damp this far inland.

> Season of mists and mellow fruitfulness,
> Close bosom-friend of the maturing sun . . .

He was alone for a while, because Brown had gone off to Bedhampton for three weeks to visit Dilke's relatives. Keats was surprised to discover how much he enjoyed being alone. There were fewer perplexities, more subtle freedoms, such as studying his own face in the glass to search out signs of the cowardice that he felt at not having gone to Hampstead to see Fanny Brawne. He could not make himself go. It would have been "venturing into a fire." He was indeed a coward; he could not "bear the pain of being happy."

Yet, solitude, despite this guilt, made possible "the sweet converse of an innocent mind," the poet's mind, stimulated into renewed activity by the brief hustle in London, brought to fulfillment by flight from its poisonous air, back to the rural countryside,

> With fruit the vines that round the thatch-eaves run;
> To bend with apples the moss'd cottage-trees,
>   And fill all fruit with ripeness to the core;
>   To swell the gourd, and plump the hazel shells
> With a sweet kernel; to set budding more,
>   And still more, later flowers for the bees,
>   Until they think warm days will never cease,
>   For Summer has o'er-brimm'd their clammy cells.

In spite of the chill air, the autumn was rich with its half-reaped furrow, the winnowing wind, the gleaner, the cider press . . .

> Where are the songs of Spring? Ay, where are they?
>   Think not of them, thou hast thy music too,—
> While barred clouds bloom the soft-dying day,
>   And touch the stubble-plains with rosy hue;
> Then in a wailful choir the small gnats mourn
>   Among the river sallows, borne aloft
>   Or sinking as the light wind lives or dies;
> And full-grown lambs loud bleat from hilly bourn;
>   Hedge-crickets sing; and now with treble soft
> The red-breast whistles from a garden-croft;
>   And gathering swallows twitter in the skies.

The world was to be blessed with one more Keatsian ode, "To Autumn."

This brief solitude was both fruitful and clarifying. His thoughts and plans were coming into realistic focus, not in terms of far-fetched adventures on ships plying between England and India, but of a solitary room in the heart of London, there to live and write and find employment of a journalistic sort. He had borrowed from Brown too much; there was to be no more of that. He would not go back to

Brown's bounty, nor to being separated by a wall from the woman he loved and needed and wanted. What a morbid arrangement to have fallen into!

He would write to Brown about his new plan first, of course, and then to the Dilkes, since they now lived in London, right in Westminster.

"It is quite time I should set myself doing something, and live no longer upon hopes," he told Brown. "I am getting into an idle minded, vicious way of life, almost content to live upon others. In no period of my life have I acted with any self will, but in throwing up the apothecary-profession. That I do not repent of . . . My occupation is entirely literary. . . . I will write, on the liberal side of the question, for whoever will pay me . . . I purpose living in town in a cheap lodging, and endeavoring, for a beginning, to get the theatricals of some paper. When I can afford to compose deliberate poems I will . . . Suppose the tragedy [*Otho*] should succeed, —there will be no harm done."

A pleasant picture! If their play succeeded, he'd be a writer on some journal, a successful playwright, a known poet. . . . Oh, he'd do something else for a living if he could; but he was really fit for nothing but literature.

"I think you will see the reasonableness of my plan," he wrote to Charles Dilke on the twenty-second of September, "that I may be in the reach of books and information, of which there is here a plentiful lack . . . Now I come to my request. Should you like me for a neighbor again? Come, plump it out, I won't blush . . . Therefore will you look about Marsham, or Romney Street for a couple of rooms for me . . ."

And to Dilke again on the first of October, lest he have any notion that Keats was not serious about this new plan: "That your imagination may not have time to take too great an alarm I state immediately that I want you to hire me a couple of rooms in Westminster. Quietness and cheapness are the essentials."

In another few days he was established at 25 College Street, near Westminster Abbey, the Dilkes, and St. James's Park. The British Museum, where he planned to do long hours of reading and research, was a long walk away through noisy, muddy streets, but that was all right. Oh, it was a great plan! He ought to have hit upon it a year sooner. He wrote confidently of his new arrangement to his publishers. They could expect him to be more productive in the future!

He did not immediately call upon any of the journals for which he hoped to work. He must set his house to rights first and endeavor to reduce to a minimum the time-consuming chores, chores that Brown had always tended to. Next he must write a great many notes to friends letting them know of his new location.

Joseph Severn appeared at his door almost at once, delighted to see the long-absent Keats.

"My dear fellow, I'm so happy you are to be in London."

Keats's spirits soared at once, and Severn's visit lasted all afternoon and into the evening. They expanded together in a torrent of talk and at length settled down while Severn listened and Keats read him everything he had written since their last meeting. Severn found his odes delightful, but he did not care for *Lamia*, and he was distressed to learn that Keats had given up *Hyperion*.

When Severn left him, Keats's energy drained away. Once again he became a tormented prey to lassitude and longing. He held the inside of his wrist against his forehead—too hot! He felt his own pulse—too fast! He looked at his writing table—too far away!

He must rest a day or two before calling on any periodicals about employment. No doubt Hazlitt could direct him. But he must rest first, must be in good appearance . . .

Idleness generated loneliness and desire. He listened, breath suspended, for the tinkle of a pianoforte and heard only the noises of the London streets. He thought of the merriment of teatime around Mrs. Brawne's table, because he heard merry children beneath his window. Who was at the tea table? How many young men would be milling about Fanny at Christmastime? Were she and her mother going to balls? Jealousy and doubt swept over him. He had been away too long, and he could not stay away from her any longer. He ought to have gone to Hampstead that last time in London.

On the morning that he boarded a stage for Hampstead, he had been in his London quarters only a week, but the week seemed like a millennium. The fine, cool weather of early October gave him a little zest, and the sight of Wentworth Place—at long last—added more. He hurried down the lane and across the yard, reaching eagerly for the knocker, and when the door was pulled open he rushed into the warm and excited welcome like a traveler fleeing indoors from a storm.

She still loved him. Her mother was cordial. There was no host of other young men in the room. Fanny seemed not nearly so coquettish as in the past. She held out her arms to him as though she had been relieved of fears herself.

It had been a good idea after all, this brief visit, because it restored his resolve, and he was able to return to College Street determined to stay with his plan for earning a living.

"My sweet Girl," he wrote to Fanny Brawne the very next morning. "I am living today in yesterday. I was in a complete fascination all day. I feel myself at your mercy. Write me ever so few lines and tell me you will forever be less kind to me than yesterday. You dazzled me. There is nothing in the world so bright and delicate . . ."

But two days later he still had not mustered sufficient strength to trudge about town calling on editors. He was losing his powers of self-discipline even in daylight hours,

and there was nothing to his thoughts now but a single compelling longing for Fanny, Fanny, Fanny.

"My dearest Girl, This moment I have set myself to copy
some verses out fair. I cannot proceed with any degree of
content. I must write you a line or two and see if that will
assist in dismissing you from my mind for ever so short a time.
Upon my soul I can think of nothing else. The time is passed
when I had power to advise and warn you against the unpromising morning of my life. My love has made me selfish.
I cannot exist without you. I am forgetful of everything
but seeing you again. My life seems to stop there. I see no
further. You have absorbed me . . . My sweet Fanny, will
your heart never change? My love, will it? I have no limit
now to my love . . ."

> The day is gone, and all its sweets are gone!
>   Sweet voice, sweet lips, soft hand, and softer breast,
> Warm breath, light whisper, tender semi-tone,
>   Bright eyes, accomplish'd shape, and lang'rous waist!

The day—the short visit to her—made remaining in London
impossible. There was no other thing for him to do than to
return to Wentworth Place. Brown and the Dilkes rallied to
him, and he moved from College Street to quarters with the
Dilkes until Brown could arrange for him at Wentworth
Place. On the twentieth of October, he was back at Hampstead. There he had Brown to give him loving supervision,
Brown to take care of all the housekeeping details, Brown to
do his copying for him, to assure him that as soon as he had
finished making a copy of *Otho* it would be ready to show
producers at Drury Lane. And he had the almost won "fair
melody, kind siren";

> O let me sip that tear!
> And whisper one sweet word that I may know
> This is this world . . .

Mrs. Brawne seemed more compassionate in her attitude on this returning to Hampstead, and into her compassion he read the beginning of consent. Perhaps she felt encouraged by the prospect of a play at Drury Lane, and perhaps by the new poem he and Brown were beginning to discuss.

He and Brown had been talking at random, and Brown lightly dropped into the conversation the idea of a "comic faery poem." Keats thought the Spenserian stanza would suit it best, and Brown encouraged him to begin. "The Cap and Bells, or, The Jealousies," was to be its title. No heavy literary effort, this was to be dashed off with a loose wrist, a satirical thing, aimed at popular appeal, and Keats was to use a pen name for it, Lucy Vaughan Lloyd.

Here in the healing country air his health began to return and he recovered enough strength to work for two or three hours each morning. "Cap and Bells" moved along swiftly, the phrases and verses and rhymes falling into place with ease, and by the seventeenth of November Keats was confident enough of it to write to Taylor and Hessey, "I have come to a determination not to publish anything I have now ready written; but for all that to publish a poem before long and that I hope to make a fine one. . . . Two or three such poems, if God should spare me, written in the course of the next six years, would be a famous gradus ad Parnassum altissimum. I mean they would nerve me up to the writing of a few fine plays—my greatest ambition."

He was fully justified in aiming his ambitions toward drama, because Brown returned from London one day to tell him that Drury Lane wanted to produce *Otho*. They planned to hold it over until next season, though, and so Keats and his collaborator agreed to take it elsewhere. Keats needed the money now.

Cheerfully he returned to his short stint of work each morning, taking a leisurely dinner, and walking and resting in the afternoon. Life with Brown now consisted of "break-fast, dinner (not tea for we have left that off), supper, sleep, confab, stirring the fire and reading."

In the gray December weather Keats looked out upon a bleak garden, a scattering of withered leaves, an empty night-ingale's nest, shriveled heads of flowers that had not been cut before they perished. The sight made him feel weary, ex-tremely weary, and the room seemed chilly. His throat felt sore and rough again, and the hacking cough was increasing in frequency. Brown insisted that he consult a doctor, but the doctor found nothing wrong with Keats, merely recom-mended that he purchase a warm greatcoat and a pair of thick shoes to wear when he went out.

Keats did as he was told, but the coat did not cure his weariness, and work on "Cap and Bells" was beginning to lag because of it. Keats, the licensed apothecary, thought of an expedient. He went quietly up to London one day and pur-chased a small bottle of laudanum. He knew how to handle it; he understood it; he would take just a drop or two to sus-tain himself through a few hours of creative writing. He would be careful . . . so very careful . . .

Under the influence of the first dosage, false energy coursed through his system, his head cleared, his imagination grew bright, and language was his to command. He wrote at high speed while the effect of the drug lasted, laying down his pen at last in a secret triumph, fully prepared for the devastating fatigue that would follow in its wake. But he understood what he was doing. He would endure the fatigue for the rest of the day—until tomorrow morning—then just another drop or two—and when "Cap and Bells" was completed he would stop using laudanum, his situation solved.

Perhaps he could finish the poem before Christmas. He had already accepted an invitation to spend that day with the Dilkes, and he had promised his sister a visit before Christmas.

By the twenty-second of December he knew he would have to break his promise to his sister. "I am sorry to say I have been and continue rather unwell, and therefore shall not be able to promise certainly," he wrote to her.

"Cap and Bells" was still not completed, and to maintain his morning output he had to increase his dosage. His hand holding the bottle was arrested in midair by an angry, frightened, shocked voice.

"Keats! My dear Keats! What is that? What are you doing?"

Charles Armitage Brown had entered unexpectedly, rushing forward to seize Keats's wrist and take the bottle from him.

"You are a doctor! You know the danger of such a thing!"

For a brief instant Keats saw himself through his friend's eyes and was shocked by his own desperate stupidity.

"I promise you," he whispered without looking up. "I promise you that I shall never touch it again."

"I know that you will not," Brown replied. "I know that nothing will induce you to break your word once given."

They never afterward spoke of the incident, and Keats—staring morning after morning at the untouched and unfinished manuscript—spiraled down into acute misery. He was but a voice. His life was but the life of winds and tides.

CHAPTER XII

Go Thou to Rome

SLOWLY HE FOUGHT HIS WAY back up toward the surface, but the surface seemed out of reach of his feeble efforts. Melancholy drove him down. His irritability increased—grew worse when he heard Fanny and Charles Armitage Brown laughing and talking together. His melancholy and his irritability were beginning to render him helpless against waves of jealousy.

> I cry your mercy—pity—love!—aye, love!
>   Merciful love that tantalises not,
> One-thoughted, never-wandering, guileless love,
>   Unmask'd, and being seen—without a blot!
> O! let me have thee whole,—all—all—be mine!
>   That shape, that fairness, that sweet minor zest
> Of love, your kiss,—those hands, those eyes divine,
>   That warm, white, lucent, million-pleasured breast,—
> Yourself—your soul—in pity give me all,
>   Withhold no atom's atom or I die . . .

What did lift him out of his despondency for a little while

was the news that his brother George had decided to return to England to have the money question out with Abbey. George had been gone a year-and-a-half, and he had been less generous about his letter writing than John. Waiting for him and for all the news he would bring about his life in the dense forests of the wilderness among copper-colored aborigines worked John into a mild elation. And he had news for George! His new volume of poems was to come out after all. *Lamia, Isabella, The Eve of St. Agnes,* his odes and some other pieces were to come out as a book this next summer.

George Keats reached England early in January of 1820, and at first sight of him John could not discern why he seemed different until he realized that it was the cut of his clothing as well as the change in his physical appearance. A more severe climate had given George a lean, wiry figure and made him more energetic. Suddenly John did not feel like his own brother's father, because George was so much more mature, appraising him at the same time.

"You're thinner," George said. "You look more like Tom than I ever realized."

Too much time had elapsed, the brothers discovered almost at once, and too many vastly different experiences had intervened. They embraced once on meeting and that was all. To widen the breach further, George did not take kindly to Fanny Brawne, and Fanny was acutely aware of it.

John Keats's rapidly worsening physical condition made it impossible for him to conceal his resentment of George's disapproval. He struggled against the demons of melancholia and jealousy to sustain some degree of cheerfulness for his brother, and distrust and suspicion soon joined the other demons. George had come to England for money, and he and John had some tight-lipped conferences with Abbey over their mismanaged financial situation. Under pressure Abbey did discover that there were some securities that could be converted into cash, and George was frank to remind Abbey that since Tom's death the interest of the remaining three heirs must be larger. When George suggested that he take all the cash now available to himself as well as John back to America for investment in another riverboat project, John began to feel pushed about and abused. George must want to break his heart altogether! George must want to ruin him!

"He's taking only eight hundred pounds," Brown tried to reason with Keats. "And America is a land where an investment can mushroom quickly."

"He doesn't want me to marry Fanny! He's taking the money away so that I can't."

"I don't think that enters into it, Keats. I'm sure it does not."

"You know he dislikes Fanny . . ."

"Look, my dear fellow. George really loves you. He is making copies of a host of your poems to take back with him. He knows you are a genius. He has faith in his investment, and he wants it to succeed for you as well as for himself."

John Keats was quieted but not convinced, and in a morbid blue mood he sat staring glumly out of the window. A quiet snow had begun to fall, covering all of Hampstead Heath in a blanket of delicate white.

George left for Liverpool to take ship for America on the twenty-eighth of January, 1820, and his final decision was to take only seven hundred pounds with him and leave the other hundred with John. The hundred was a mere fragment of the debts John was gradually accumulating, and after George's departure John fingered the bank notes ruefully as though he doubted the quality of their texture. Well, George was gone and he had managed to keep up more or less while George was present, traveling with him to Walthamstow and to London. Perhaps this meant that he was stronger than he realized. Perhaps he ought to get back to "Cap and Bells."

John Keats felt even more confident of his energies as the winter turned unnaturally warm toward the end of January and the snow melted from sight. On the third of February, a deceptively mild day, he boarded the stage to London. He'd take advantage of this fair weather, visit a few friends, chat with his publisher about his forthcoming volume of poems, and generally have a day of it. The day proved interesting, taxing, long, stretching late into the evening, and the return stage he finally boarded would not bring him home until eleven. With his usual habit of economy he rode outside, without benefit of the greatcoat which the sunny day had lured him into leaving at home, and the chill damp night air closed in around him. His jacket seemed like paper; he began to shiver and to feel wretched out of pure fear of the effect.

The coach careened and rocked and sent waves of nausea through his system. He began to cough and as quickly the cough became muffled by a quantity of fluid in his throat—the taste of blood!—followed by the feeling of suffocation. His shivering ceased and he became warm, impervious to the cold air, fevered, exhilarated, and he knew what it had to mean. Upon his conscious understanding burst the fact of his health that he had blinded himself to for so long. He was to follow his mother—Tom—Ah, no, no, no!

He leaped down from the stage at his destination and rushed wildly into the house.

"What is the matter?" Brown asked, jumping up. "You are fevered?"

"Yes, yes. I was on the outside of the stage this bitter night till I was severely chilled, but now I don't feel it. Fevered! Of course, a little."

Brown behaved as though he too had realized for some time. This was all so clear! Brown suggested that he go straight to bed, supported him up the stairs, helped him un-

dress and slip between the cold sheets. A paroxysm of coughing seized Keats and more fluid rushed to his mouth.

"Bring me a candle, Brown," he asked as soon as he could
speak. "Let me see this blood."

Brown obeyed and they both examined the brilliant red
spot on the sheet.

"I know the color of that blood," said Keats. "It is arterial
blood. I cannot be deceived by that color. That drop of
blood is my death warrant. I must die."

Brown rushed out of the house in quest of a doctor, and
came back with one very soon after. True to the best medical
knowledge of the times, the physician opened a vein in Keats's
arm and relieved him of still more blood, advised him to rest
in bed a few days, and departed with no show of alarm, having declared categorically that there was nothing wrong with
his lungs.

"Fanny!" Keats whispered to Brown. "I want to see her."

"It is very late," Brown told him. "Try to sleep."

Brown drew a chair to Keats's bedside and sat perfectly
still, watching and waiting for Keats to sleep.

Keats was physically weakened, but his brain had been
shocked into wakefulness by his own diagnosis of his condition. Dearest Fanny, sweet love, how long will it be before
you are released of your bondage to me? A week? A month?
A year?

He did not fall asleep until five in the morning, and when
he opened his eyes once more the room seemed vaguely
strange and vaguely familiar, flooded with the light of late
morning. Brown still sat where Keats had last seen him, his
head fallen forward in sleep.

"Fanny," Keats whispered, and Brown was wide awake.

"She has gone out, Keats," he whispered back. "She will
be here later."

"Don't tell her that I have the consumption."

"The doctor finds nothing wrong with your lungs."

"He is mistaken."

"Rest quietly."

"I am too weak to get up."

"Don't worry about anything, Keats. In a little while I'll bring you some breakfast, and later I'll help you shave."

The breakfast that his friend brought would have nourished a nightingale but nothing larger, since the prevailing viewpoint called for starvation diet in time of illness. The tea, at least, gave Keats a modicum of stimulation.

After he had rested from the effort of eating, Keats asked for pen and paper, and fearing to disturb the patient by thwarting him Brown complied with his request.

"Dearest Fanny," Keats wrote. "I shall send this the moment you return. They say I must remain confined to this room for some time. The consciousness that you love me will make a pleasant prison of the house next to yours. You must come and see me frequently: this evening, without fail—when you must not mind about my speaking in a low tone for I am ordered to do so though I can speak out. Yours ever, sweetest love—J. Keats."

And to his sister he wrote a minimizing account of his illness, suggesting that if he were laid up long Abbey might give her permission to come and see him. Everyone was ill just now, he reminded her, what with colds, fevers, and such.

He really did have a sign and sense of recovery after a few days in bed. By the sixth day, he was carried downstairs and placed on a sofa in the front parlor—the room opposite his own parlor—so that he could look out over Hampstead Heath, and in another few days he was permitted to walk about the room. No air though! Fresh air was injurious.

With the feeling of recovery his own hope returned. A lung might heal; not everyone who had consumption died of it. On the tenth of February he wrote to his fiancée, "I shall be looking forward to health and the spring and a regular routine of our old walks." And to his sister, after a very fine day had relaxed the no-fresh-air rule, "Yesterday morning being very fine I took a walk for a quarter of an hour in the garden and was very much refresh'd by it."

Fanny Brawne, Charles Armitage Brown, and the increasingly sympathetic Mrs. Brawne were his only companions during February, and their combined optimism was stimulated by their love for the patient more than by good judgment, for they allowed him too much liberty. In the first week of March John Keats was stricken with violent and persistent heart palpitations and had to be helped back into bed.

Brown had had enough of local doctors. He summoned Dr. Robert Bree from Hanover Square, London. Bree had received his medical degree from Oxford University, had had years of experience as an army doctor in a variety of countries, and was prominent in the Royal College of Physicians and the Royal Society. But Dr. Bree's diagnosis rather supported that of the local man: Keats had "no pulmonary affection, no organic defect whatever."

"I assure you, Mr. Keats, that you are suffering from nervous irritability. You have been worrying about too many things in recent years, and your poetry excites you too much."

Keats believed him for a while, because he so earnestly wanted to, and he worked conscientiously at resting and doing nothing, spending most of his day lying down.

"If you would have me recover, flatter me with a hope of happiness when I shall be well," he said to Brown, "for I am now so weak that I can be flattered into hope."

Too often when he opened his eyes after dozing he saw Fanny and his friend side by side, exchanging smiles and glances, and his sick imagination tortured him with misinterpretations. Conscience-smitten by what he knew was his own illness, he included in a short note to Fanny, "any organic derangement always occasions a phantasmagoria."

By the middle of March he was moving about cautiously again, working for short periods on the final revisions of *Lamia*, but overexertion brought on attacks of palpitation. He studied Dr. Bree's face each time the physician called, and built his hopes on the doctor's optimistic smile of pleasure in his progress.

"I should like to go up to town soon," Keats suggested.

"I can think of no reason to forbid it," the doctor replied.

On the twenty-fifth of March, a Saturday, John Keats did venture successfully to London—to attend the first official showing of Haydon's picture, "Christ's Entry into Jerusalem." The huge canvas that had taken six years to complete was hanging in a second-floor room of the garish Egyptian Hall in the Piccadilly section of London. The fabulous Haydon, in debt to everyone, had hired the hall for a year, planning to present his picture at an invitation affair and then charge admission in the future.

Keats and Haydon had become more or less reconciled after their quarrel over money, although the old free intimacy had gone out of their friendship, and the large crowd of fashionable and prominent persons who came to the debut of the painting made their meeting easy. Haydon was so excited and so busy receiving his guests that he and Keats could exchange only a few words.

And there was Hazlitt! Keats began to experience the boyish exuberance of a class reunion as he wrung the hand of the middle-aged critic and popular lecturer. Hazlitt, too, had come to see his own head in the painting. Hazlitt's joy at seeing Keats was a tonic to the sick man, and they remained together, working their way through the crowd to a bench near a wall and watched the public reactions to "Christ's Entry."

Hazlitt jostled Keats with his elbow and pointed discreetly

toward the Persian ambassador in his brilliantly colored silks. The high point of the afternoon was the appearance of the beautiful and dignified actress, who had retired, Mrs. Siddons. With the sweep of a graceful hand she pre-empted the room for her stage, paused before the painting, and spoke her lines, "It is decidedly successful! The paleness gives it an awful and supernatural look." A thrill went through the gathering to hear the voice of the great tragedienne once more.

"That will bring in the paying public," chuckled Hazlitt. "Now the faults in the picture will be forgotten."

Keats returned to Hampstead feeling a month advanced in his recovery and went immediately to bed to rest in happy penance. He could see his own feeling of well-being reflected in Fanny's face as she bent over him and held his hand against the bosom of her dress.

Brown waited for a day when Keats felt particularly well— and calm—to give him the news of *Otho's* fate at Covent Garden. Covent Garden had turned it down—and they had burned their own bridges behind them at Drury Lane! There was no other producing theater in London. Well . . . there had to be a few "deformed thoughts and feelings" at this news . . . *Otho* was to have solved his financial worries . . . There was only one wise thing to do now and that was to concentrate on his forthcoming volume of verse. Perhaps next winter he and Brown could write another play.

Meanwhile the summer was ahead of them and must be planned for, since Brown wanted to sublet his half of the house as usual. Brown was considering seriously another walking tour in Scotland. Keats and Brown were both startled when, on an April day, Dr. Bree jovially advised Keats to go to Scotland with Brown.

"Do accompany him, Mr. Keats," Dr. Bree insisted. "The exercise and change of air will be most beneficial."

Keats and Brown needed only to exchange a glance to decide against such a foolhardy adventure. Keats knew he wasn't really well. In a letter to his sister he had said, "I should think myself quite well were I not reminded every now and then by faintness and a tightness in the chest."

To Brown he said, "I rather feel that the doctor is not familiar with the Scottish Highlands."

Brown nodded, and went ahead to make plans for traveling alone. He was to take a coastwise smack up to a Scottish port and set out on foot from there.

Although Keats's illness had considerably reduced his social activities, it had not cut him off from his friends, and the people who had known him the longest were the most devoted. His once literary mentor, Leigh Hunt, suggested that for the summer he take rooms near him in Kentish Town, another suburban village lying almost midway between Hampstead and London. The Hunts had moved to 13 Mortimer Terrace in Kentish Town, and they found Keats a room just a short walk away at 2 Wesleyan Place. With Brown's help he transferred his few belongings and his books to Wesleyan Place, and the bustle and activity stimulated him somewhat as his visit to Egyptian Hall had done. He was really a very short distance from Wentworth Place!

But his moods during the past year had been infecting Fanny's personality more than he realized, and now and again a somberness clouded her gay disposition. This day she looked anxiously at him and asked,

"Will you return to Wentworth Place in the fall?"

He had not thought of not returning. What did she see in his face? What did she sense?

"Always wear my ring," she begged.

Of course he would! What an easy promise to give!

They clung to each other, and Brown with a little show of impatience strove to lure Keats away from the exaggerated farewell.

"Why not sail the first short leg of my trip with me?" Brown suggested. "The air will be bracing."

Keats went aboard the sailing vessel at the London dock and enjoyed several quiet hours on deck as the boat found its cautious way down the Thames to Gravesend, where the river widens into the North Sea. There he clasped Brown's hand in farewell, accepted fifty pounds that Brown insisted he take, exchanged promises with his friend to write, and went ashore—to look for the stage that would take him back to London and there to take a second stage out Highgate Road to the short street that turned off it.

Number two Wesleyan Place was one in a row of four two-story attached stone houses; its street floor had two arch-topped windows and a door and its upper-floor windows were graced by black iron balconies. Keats's room was on the street level in the front.

When he entered the high-ceilinged room he found the grate in the fireplace cold, because he had not been expected, and the chill combined with fatigue to send his spirits plummeting down. He was lonely, lonely! He had just left Fanny Brawne, had just said good-by to Charles Armitage Brown; he was in no mood to go calling in the confused household of the Hunts where boisterous children created a bedlam. He found a candle and struggled with tinder and strips of wood coated with sulphur until he lit it. Its rays spread through the room revealing on the table a vase of fresh wild flowers. From whom? From whom? From Fanny! Fanny Brawne!

He sank down into a chair before the cold vacant staring eye of the fireplace and gave way to despair. He was sick! Dying! No, no, *no!* He was recovering. This was just a brief summer interlude. In the late fall he'd return to Went-worth Place, as soon as Brown returned. But there had been a deep fear in Fanny's eyes when he left her, a fear based on knowledge. What had she seen in his face?

John Keats was profoundly ill—in his heart he knew it—
and his mind was rapidly becoming as ill as his body—and
he almost realized this too. Once more absence was anything
but a solution, and the demons of imaginary jealousy assumed
control. He wanted to let Fanny alone, to free her from
bondage to himself, but at the same time he needed her for
himself and could not bear the thought of her being with
anyone else. Where was she now? With *whom?* He could
walk out there any afternoon and be sure, but cunningly he
knew he must not let her see into his state of mind at the
moment.

He resisted the temptation to write to her while he felt
so morbid, and instead he went to bed and let the bevy of
phantoms and specters take command. Next morning, he
awakened feeling refreshed by a few hours sleep, and bol-
stered by hot tea he decided to rest and later in the day to
write Fanny a pleasant note.

"My dearest Girl: I endeavour to make myself as patient
as possible. Hunt amuses me very kindly. Besides, I have
your ring on my finger and your flowers on the table. I shall
not expect to see you yet because it would be so much pain
to part from you again. When the books you want come
you shall have them. I am very well this afternoon."

A writer must write to know that "this is this world," and
he had written nothing but an occasional note since his hemorrhage four months ago. But he felt too tired during his
first few days at his new place, and he needed more time to
adjust to the change of environment. He attempted to read,
but every line he read spoke of love in some way—avowals
of love, unrequited love, betrayed love—heroes snatched away
by circumstances, heroines like Cressida forgetting their vows
of devotion the moment their lovers were out of sight.

Self-pity and suspicion took hold of him and became so
real he lost all power to conceal them from others, and upon

Fanny Brawne fell the burden of his mental anguish during his first weeks in Kentish Town.

"My dearest Girl," he wrote to her. "I know it may give you a little pain, because I wish you to see how unhappy I am for love of you, and endeavour as much as I can to entice you to give up your whole heart to me whose whole existence hangs upon you. You could not step or move an eyelid but it would shoot to my heart. I am greedy of you. Do not think of any thing but me. Do not live as if I was not existing. Do not forget me. But have I any right to say you forget me? Perhaps you think of me all day. Have I any right to wish you to be unhappy for me? . . . Your going to town alone, when I heard of it was a shock to me—yet I expected it—*promise me you will not for some time, till I get better*. Promise me this and fill the paper full of the most endearing names. . . . Well you may exclaim, how selfish, how cruel, not to let me enjoy my youth! To wish me to be unhappy! You must be so if you love me—upon my soul I can be contented with nothing else. If you could really what is call'd enjoy yourself at a party—if you can smile in people's faces, and wish them to admire you *now*, you never have nor ever will love me. . . . No—my sweet Fanny—I am wrong. I do not want you to be unhappy—and yet I do, I must while there is so sweet a beauty—my loveliest my darling! Good bye! I kiss you—O the torments!"

The healthy, normal, nineteen-year-old Fanny wrote the best reply she knew how. Why did he ill treat her with words? Why did he not come across the Heath and visit her?

Oh, he was bitterly sorry, he replied. "My dearest love, I am afraid to see you, I am strong but not strong enough to see you. Will my arm ever be round you again. And if so shall I be obliged to leave you again. My sweet Love!" But the pen was in his hand and his hand was guided by a sick and tortured mind, and another cruel and distorted letter resulted, more revealing in its content than its predecessor. "My friends have behaved well to me in every instance but one, and there they have become tattlers, and inquisitors into my conduct: spying upon a secret I would rather die than share it with any body's confidence. For this I cannot wish them well, I care not to see any of them again. If I am the theme, I will not be the friend of idle gossips. Good gods what a shame it is our loves should be so put into the microscope of a coterie. . . . These laughers, who do not like you, who envy you for your beauty, who would have God-bless'd-me from you for ever: who were plying me with disencouragements with respect to you eternally. People are revengeful—do not mind them—do nothing but love me. . . . I wish to believe in immortality—I wish to live with you forever. . . ."

He was surrounded by more love and understanding than he could possibly have comprehended, and occasionally the "inquisitors" and "tattlers" drew him into a social gathering or mustered their generous patience and paid him a visit. His editors came in for their share of suspicion, and as he went over the printers' proofs of his new volume of poetry he frequently detected gratuitous alterations in his verses, alterations that utterly destroyed his intended meaning. Did he really want this book to come out? He wasn't sure. Where would the strength come from to read the Tory reviews?

From George in America came a letter in the middle of June filled with family woes and problems. George's daughter was gravely ill. One of these days George was going to send John two hundred pounds, but he couldn't do it just yet.

In the depths of it all John Keats received an alarming letter from his sister in Walthamstow asking him to come and see her at once. It was urgent, she insisted.

He responded as he always had when some member of his family needed him: he grew excited and concerned, forgot his own limitations, and planned to visit her next day. After a fitful, worry-filled night, he started out in the early morning down Wesleyan Place toward Highgate Road to await the stage, but he was suddenly stopped in his tracks by a fit of coughing that brought a rush of blood into his throat and mouth. His head spun from the effort and the realization, and swaying slightly he found his way back to his room and fell on the bed face down.

> Stung
> And poisoned was my spirit: despair sung
> A war song of defiance 'gainst all hell.
> A hand was at my shoulder to compel . . .

Waves of nausea swept over him, and the hand on his shoulder became heavier—real—and he opened his eyes to discover that it was the housemaid to tidy the room.

"Mr. Keats?"

When he turned on his back he saw her stifle a gasp at the sight of his face.

"Do not worry," he told her. "I didn't sleep well."

Perturbed and only half convinced, she withdrew.

He remained on the bed, knowing he ought to send a note to his sister, knowing he ought to summon help, but resisting every sensible thought. He decided instead to rest all day so that he could keep a social engagement with the Hunts that evening. A persistent, nervous headache stayed with him like his own shadow, but he went to the Hunts just the same, and he was glad that he had, because others had come to meet the author of *Endymion*. He could bring himself to contribute almost nothing to the conversation, but now and again he intercepted a glance stolen his way. They seemed to be satisfied with what they saw. They seemed to feel that he looked like a poet, a major poet, one who would be counted among England's poets after his death.

Returning to the barren cheerlessness of his own room, he was seized with another paroxysm of coughing—and another hemorrhage. He knew he could not keep this a secret much longer, and he lay stretched on his back, floating half way between waking and sleeping, hoping and despairing—"Upon a bow he leaned, wretched"—until the morning.

The light of a new day brought him a modicum of good judgment, and when the housemaid appeared with his tea he whispered, "Please, the Hunts . . ."

"Yes, sir!" and she was gone in a panic to bring Mrs. Hunt back in an incredibly short time.

Uncombed though she was at that early hour, Marianne Hunt displayed both efficiency and single-mindedness. John Keats was to be transferred to Mortimer Terrace, and before the end of the day she had executed her decision with full approbation of her husband.

The Hunts summoned Dr. George Darling from London, a physician with a most respectable reputation and known to Keats's publishers. Like his professional predecessors, Dr. Darling further bled the patient and left him weak and re-sistless, but he did at least take a less optimistic view of Keats's condition than Dr. Bree. An ardent advocate of the virtues of a warm, dry climate, he suggested a trip to Italy.

Keats and everyone who loved him approved of the idea, but until the money for it could be found somewhere he con-tinued as an invalid in the home of the Hunts. He did manage to send his sister a short note explaining his failure to visit her, but he did not attempt to write to Fanny Brawne for another two weeks.

Meanwhile, around the first of July, 1820, he received ad-vanced copies of his new book, *Lamia, Isabella, The Eve of*

St. Agnes, and Other Poems. He fondled the light tan volume with a limp and indifferent hand. It was slightly larger than the *Poems* of 1817, although considerably thicker, but still small enough to slip into a man's pocket. To be told that Mr. Taylor had said that "if it does not sell well, I think nothing will ever sell well again," left Keats lifeless. At least he would not have to read the reviews for several more weeks.

This last attack had relieved him of some of his worst psychotic demons for a while, and when he wrote to Fanny Brawne—a short note on the fourth and a longer letter on the fifth of July—he was almost rational, even gentle, although still somewhat erratic and jealous.

"My dearest Girl, I have been [for] a walk this morning with a book in my hand, but as usual I have been occupied with nothing but you: I wish I could say in an agreeable manner. I am tormented day and night. They talk of my going to Italy. 'Tis certain I shall never recover. . . ." The letter referred cruelly to her "flirtations" with Brown.

Dr. Darling persisted in the recommendation of a warm, dry climate, and Dr. William Lambe, who lived in Kentish Town, was soon called in for consultation. He concurred with Darling. Keats must find a way to go to Italy and remain there during the English winter.

During the middle of July Joseph Severn paid Keats a visit, and when he saw Keats's appearance he promised to continue his visits once or twice a week.

Reviews of *Lamia* began to come in during July and continued during August, September, and October. In them it was clear that the literary tide had turned. They ranged from passionately partisan in the independent periodicals to mildly critical in one or two Tory magazines. Apparently the artificially induced assault on the "Cockney School" had grown stale; critics who had foreseen Keats's future in his earlier works were now ecstatic, and attackers of *Endymion* began to eat crow. Some of them, who had ignored *Endymion* when it appeared, now mended their fence posts by reviewing it together with *Lamia*. This was an artist's reward for keeping faith with himself, not always realized in his own lifetime.

Sales of the volume were not immediately large, but they would grow in time. Keats was among the English poets now, and he would remain there.

His feeble energies stirred at the encouragement of the reviews and at the gratification in the faces of those who loved him and had been first to recognize his importance as an artist. He had been gaining strength, he knew, and perhaps death could be forestalled a little while if he took the doctor's advice and spent the English winter in Italy.

He quailed a little at the thought of saying another farewell to Fanny Brawne, but perhaps she would endeavor to make it easy for him. He would visit her soon.

As he lay resting on his bed one warm day in early August, he heard what sounded like a caller at the door downstairs, but the Hunt home was such a center of activity, filled with comings and goings, that he did not feel curious enough to stir himself. Not until the next day did he find out what it was when Leigh Hunt's oldest boy brought him a letter from Fanny with the seal on it broken. It had arrived the day before.

"Marianne!" cried Keats to Mrs. Hunt. "Why did you do this? Why was my letter from Fanny withheld from me?"

Mrs. Hunt was dumbfounded. She had given it to the maid to take upstairs to him, she explained. The maid had given it to him only now, the boy added.

"But the seal! How did that become broken? Someone is spying on my mail!"

It did Marianne and Leigh Hunt no good to plead with him

that it was an accident. He would not be quieted. His emotions mounted until he gave way to weeping.

"I am going to see her! I must go and explain to her! I am going to Wentworth Place."

"Oh, no, Keats! Rest a bit. In a day or two we will engage a carriage and drive over."

He was deaf to all reason, and he set out across the Heath. It was a short walk for a well man, but far too much for a man in Keats's condition, and he was close to fainting when he reached his destination.

Both Brawne women stretched out their arms to support him into the house and assist him upstairs to bed. He must remain with them! They were going to take care of him. His head sank into the pillow—lower—lower—

"Mother!" he whispered to the blurred image that bent over him. He must scurry out of the hedgerow back to the house to Mother—Mother—

Mrs. Brawne nursed and mothered him back to some semblance of recovery, until he could sit propped up on pillows, and before long he was able to leave the bedroom, even take short walks in the air.

Fanny seemed radiant whenever she looked at him. He was aware of the glow of happiness that seemed to surround her even before he was able to get up, whenever she brought him a tray or read to him or simply sat near him. When he was strong enough to hear it she told him why.

"My mother has consented to our marriage. As soon as you return from Italy and are well again, I shall be your wife and you will live with us. Mama loves you as much as I do now."

He held out his arms to her—

> Ah! dearest love, sweet home of all my fears,
>   And hopes, and joys, and panting miseries,—

> To-night, if I may guess, thy beauty wears
> A smile of such delight,
> As brilliant and as bright . . .

Persistently both Fanny and her mother strove to build up his hope and will to recover, encouraging him to go on with his plans for the Italian trip. Money was the only barrier, really, and he queried Abbey about it. Abbey was adamant about releasing any more funds. The only other source Keats could turn to was his publishers, and he began to negotiate with them about sale of his copyrights.

The gravity of Keats's condition and the need for the trip to Italy had become known to the whole grapevine of romantic writers, and at about the time he made his hasty trip to Wentworth Place, Keats received a letter from Percy Bysshe Shelley in Pisa, Italy, dated July 27, 1820:

"My dear Keats: I hear with great pain the dangerous accident that you have undergone, and Mr. Gisborne [a friend of the Hunts] who gives me the account of it, adds, that you continue to wear a consumptive appearance. This consumption is a disease particularly fond of people who write such good verses as you have done, and with the assistance of an English winter it can often indulge its selection;—I do not think that young and amiable poets are at all bound to gratify its taste; they have entered into no bond with the Muses to that effect . . I think you would do well to pass the winter after so tremendous an accident in Italy . . . Mrs. Shelley unites with myself in urging the request, that you would take up your residence with us.— You might come by sea to Leghorn . . . which is within a few miles of us. You ought at all events to see Italy, and your health, which I suggest as a motive, might be an excuse to you. . . . I have lately read your *Endymion* again and ever with a new sense of the treasures of poetry it contains. . . . I feel persuaded that you are capable of the greatest things, so you but will. I always tell Ollier to send you copies of my books. 'Prometheus Unbound' I imagine you will receive nearly at the same time of this letter . . . Yours sincerely, P. B. Shelley."

Keats knew he would be safe and comfortable in the care of the open-hearted Shelley; yet, even though his attitude toward the young aristocrat had mellowed considerably, he did not want to be Shelley's guest in Pisa. By the sixteenth of August, when he had been with the Brawnes nearly a week, he felt able to write Shelley a courteous reply:

"My dear Shelley: I am very much gratified that you, in a foreign country, and with a mind almost over occupied, should write to me in the strain of the letter beside me. If I do not take advantage of your invitation it will be prevented by a circumstance I have very much at heart to prophesy. There is no doubt that an English winter would put an end to me, and do so in a lingering hateful manner, therefore I must either voyage or journey to Italy as a soldier marches up to a battery. My nerves at present are the worst part of me, yet they feel soothed when I think that come what extreme may, I shall not be destined to remain in one spot long enough to take a hatred of any four particular bed-posts. I am glad you take any pleasure in my poor poem."

Keats had been reading Shelley's tragedy, *The Cenci*, and he indulged in some comment about it.

"You I am sure will forgive me for sincerely remarking that you might curb your magnanimity and be more of an artist, and 'load every rift' of your subject with ore. The thought of such discipline must fall like cold chains upon you, who perhaps never sat with your wings furl'd for six months together. And is not this extraordinary talk for the writer of *Endymion?* . . . I am in expectation of 'Prometheus' every day. . . . I remember you advising me not to publish my first-blights, on Hampstead Heath. I am returning advice upon your hands. Most of the poems in the volume I send you have been written above two years, and would never have been publish'd but from a hope of gain . . . I must express once more my deep sense of your kindness, adding my sincere thanks and respects for Mrs. Shelley. In the hope of soon seeing you I remain, Most sincerely, John Keats."

Keats had already written to Charles Armitage Brown, who was still in Scotland, telling him of his attack and relapse. "A winter in England would, I have no doubt, kill me; so I have resolved to go to Italy." Later in the month of August he was able to send Brown his exact plans, because he wanted Brown to go to Italy with him. "I ought to be off at the end of this week, as the cold winds begin to blow towards evening;—but I will wait till I have your answer to this. I am to be introduced, before I set out, to a Dr. Clark, a physician settled at Rome, who promises to befriend me in every way at Rome."

Everyone concerned waited anxiously for Brown's reply, but no word came from the man on the walking tour. Space aboard the *Maria Crowther* was engaged and her sailing date set for Sunday, September 17. Brown would come, Keats assured his friends and himself, or he would write.

"If he does not or cannot come, I shall make the journey alone," said Keats.

He was strong enough now. Had they not seen him walking on the Heath with Fanny?

On Wednesday before his sailing date, he took his leave of Fanny Brawne and her mother—another difficult farewell—everything he did seemed to increase the tightness in his chest—the room was excessively overheated—and considerately they made their embraces brief.

"Write to my sister, as often as you can," he asked Fanny, and she promised him that she would.

When he reached London he went to Taylor and Hessey's

office, planning to lodge temporarily with Taylor, and there with them he executed the docu..ient that turned over to his publishers the copyrights on his 1817 *Poems* and the *Lamia* volume and received one hundred pounds sterling in return. He had previously turned over the copyright on *Endymion* to reimburse them for the severe loss they had incurred on that unfortunate volume. His publishers assured him that as soon as losses were made up any future profits from sales of his books would be forwarded to him promptly.

"All my estate real and personal consists in the hopes of the sale of books published or unpublish'd," he told them. "Now I wish Brown and you to be the first paid creditors." This was in case of his death, and in that event would they please divide his chest of books among his friends.

On the last day before his sailing, no word had come from Brown. Sunday morning a small group of Keats's friends went with him to the dock near the Tower of London, but still Charles Armitage Brown was not among them. For a brief moment John Keats thought he really was making the voyage alone, but to his amazement he discovered that Joseph Severn had come rushing to take Brown's place on scarcely more than a day's notice.

Dear Severn! Splendid friend!

"Oh, what sights shall I see to paint in Italy!" Severn announced hopefully.

The ship was a schooner-merchantman, and as Keats and Severn stood at the rail, the sailing vessel slid away from the dock and was carried down the Thames by the tide. There was one woman passenger aboard, a Mrs. Pidgeon, and a young woman named Miss Cotterell came aboard at Gravesend. Miss Cotterell inquired in a friendly way where the two men were bound.

"We go to Rome," Keats told her.

CHAPTER XIII

Fled Is That Music

WHILE THE SHIP lay at anchor at Gravesend, a coastwise sailing smack from Dundee came up the river and furled sail nearby for a few hours. Charles Armitage Brown was aboard it, hurrying back to London in response to Keats's letters, and the two friends did not learn until much later that they had missed each other by so narrow a margin.

The *Maria Crowther* did not leave Gravesend until the afternoon and moved into a most unpromising sea. Contrary winds kept her in the Channel until the next day, and on Wednesday morning she was only off Brighton, rolling and pitching, the sea beginning to build up mountainous waves. As the sea washed into their cabin Keats rushed to rescue the books he had brought with him.

Miss Cotterell, another consumptive placing her hope in Italy, was desperately seasick and irritable when the sea was rough, charming when her *mal de mer* allowed, but often at night when the sea was bad and they were all shut in together she felt suffocated and wanted the portholes opened to give her cool air, while Keats needed them closed because the night air brought on a coughing spell and hemorrhage. Keats was not too subject to seasickness, and he did his best to create light banter and cheer the others with recitations of poetry. Even Severn, who should have been Keats's moral bulwark, was too seasick to be of much help and needed as much cheering as they.

At last, two weeks after their departure from London, the ship was anchored off the Isle of Wight in calm water, awaiting a favorable wind, and the passengers went ashore, grateful for the brief respite on solid ground. Here was a chance to post a letter to Brown!

"My dear Brown, The time has not yet come for a pleasant letter from me. I have delayed writing to you from time to time because I felt how impossible it was to enliven you with one heartening hope of my recovery; this morning in bed the matter struck me in a different matter . . . I might become too ill to write at all. . . ."

Brown, he learned too late, had been at Chichester, and he expressed his chagrin at this before going on to other subjects that agitated him. "The very thing which I want to live most for will be a great occasion of my death. I cannot help it. Who can help it? Were I in health it would make me ill, and how can I bear it in my state? I dare say you will be able to guess on what subject I am harping—you know what was my greatest pain during the first part of my illness at your house. I wish for death every day and night to deliver me from these pains, and then I wish death away, for death would destroy even those pains which are better than nothing. Land and sea, weakness and decline are great separators, but death is the great divorcer for ever. . . ."

Fanny, Fanny, Fanny . . .

"Yet the difference of my sensations with respect to Miss

Brawne and my sister is amazing. The one seems to absorb the other to a degree incredible. I seldom think of my brother and sister in America. The thought of leaving Miss Brawne is beyond every thing horrible—the sense of darkness coming over me—I eternally see her figure eternally vanishing . . ."

The stormy weather had diverted his attention, but now that the sea was calm and he could rest and reflect, he was beginning to drift down into wretchedness again.

The *Maria Crowther* finally got away from the English coast and pointed her bow toward Gibraltar, and her passengers came out on deck and enjoyed smooth sailing—until they reached the Bay of Biscay. There they ran into another storm of three days' duration, high seas washing over the ship. Keats and Severn both lay in their bunks, ill, untended, the floor awash.

At the Strait of Gibraltar where the ship moved into the calm waters of the Mediterranean, Keats appeared to recover noticeably. They sat on the deck as the sun rose behind the great rock fortress and lighted up the African coast to a brilliant gold above the sapphire blue sea. Keats watched silently as Severn tried to capture some of the scene in water colors.

But it was a false recovery. During the passage from Gibraltar to Naples Keats's gaiety vanished, and he plunged into a deep depression, coughed, hemorrhaged, ran a fever, and experienced severe sweating. When the *Maria Crowther* dropped anchor inside the breakwater at Naples and the passengers were told they must remain aboard the ship for ten days' quarantine, Keats sank down upon his bunk and closed his eyes as the breathless, humid heat of the cabin closed in around him.

Severn bathed Keats's forehead and helped him to rally himself and find his way out-of-doors. The picturesque curving harbor, the tall black cone of Vesuvius to the southward, the Apennine ridge, the ancient town with its pale pastel

buildings up the side of the slope to the northward, the color-
ful bedlam of the harbor itself, barges filled with the autumn
fruit harvest, singing and laughing stevedores with their white
teeth showing and their brown eyes flashing! This was Keats's
first experience with an exotically foreign city, and yet it left
him almost unstimulated. He wanted to be buried somewhere
near Wentworth Place, away from the glare and heat of
Naples. He could not even write to Fanny. He was afraid
to. Oh, there were coals of fire in his breast! Was he born
for this end? He could bear to die, but he could not bear to
leave her.

Severn's initiative returned now that he was freed of his
mal de mer, and he became a parent to John Keats. He took
his charge to a hotel in Naples as soon as the quarantine law
had been satisfied, and from there up the coastal road to Rome
in a small carriage. The roads along the way were unpaved,
the inns indifferent, and Keats longed only to reach his quarters. But he came to life suddenly when he realized that the
carriage was passing through the Lateran Gate of the ancient
Roman walls, and his eyes lighted up as he looked out upon
the huge, circular decaying Colosseum. They drove northward through the city over the Corso and up Via dei Condotti to Piazza di Spagna.

Dr. James Clark had found rooms for them at Number 26
Piazza di Spagna, directly across the street from his own quarters. The house (the Keats-Shelley Memorial today) is four
stories tall, square, covered with rosy-tinted plaster so typical
of Rome, its roof of fluted reddish-brown tile. It stands at the
foot of the long sweep of stone steps, the Spanish Steps, leading from the Piazza to the church at the top of the hill, Santa
Trinità dei Monti, and beyond the church spread the gardens of the Villa Borghese.

Number 26 is only two rooms wide, and Keats and Severn
had the two front rooms, two flights up. Keats occupied the

corner room with windows looking down upon both the Steps and the Piazza; Severn the slightly larger one with its single window facing the Piazza. Neither room could be called large; Keats's was about eleven feet long and less than nine feet wide, narrowing to something like six feet in front of a white marble fireplace. Its floor was paved with hexagonal red tiles that felt cool to his hot feet when he undressed and slipped into the correspondingly narrow bed. Above him the ceiling was high, decorated with small squares, each with a rose painted in it.

Even in the depths of exhaustion Keats felt that Rome would be good for him. The air was dry, the temperature pleasant. Severn's overearnestness and intense anxiety rather irked him, but he could never have achieved Rome without Severn. He wanted Severn to begin painting right away. Rome was full of ancient monuments of that culture touched off by the Greeks.

When Dr. Clark examined Keats for the first time, he expressed the opinion that Keats's chief complaint was seated in his stomach, and he prescribed rest for a while and recreation as soon as he was able. Keats knew better, so far as his symptoms were concerned, but he did experience a short and encouraging rally. During the latter part of November and the first days of December he went out upon the Spanish Steps, even toiled cautiously up them to have a good view of the big oval Barcaccia Fountain in the center of the Piazza and the Via dei Condotti beyond it. Once or twice of an infrequent evening he and Severn strolled down Via dei Condotti to the Caffè Greco. He longed to visit the Colosseum, but it was too impossibly far away.

"I am giving you a dull time of it," he said to Severn, and urged the young artist to visit the ruins and art galleries with his sketching pad; eagerly Severn obeyed.

Keats longed for a line or two of verse to pay tribute to

this city, and although he talked of beginning a long poem about the story of Sabrina, his muse was not present. He managed to write only one letter to Brown from Rome, telling Brown that it was "the most difficult thing in the world for me to write a letter. My stomach continues so bad . . . Then I am afraid to encounter the proing and conning of any thing interesting to me in England . . ."

No letters to Fanny . . . and those that came from her went unopened. He was gone away from her . . . he could never return . . . only the unprodded wound could have any hope of healing . . .

He could spend his time reading and studying a little Italian, and when Dr. Clark made the suggestion he even engaged a small saddle horse and rode out into the countryside beyond the walls. The exercise seemed helpful at the time but it proved injudicious in the long run. On the fourteenth of December, chatting with Severn in exceptionally good spirits, he was seized with a sudden coughing spell that led to a severe hemorrhage. Frantically Severn rushed for Dr. Clark, who came at once and drew more blood from the arm of the patient. Keats and the doctor stared at its unnaturally dark color.

Hysterically Keats leaped from the bed and cried, "This day shall be my last!"

It required the combined strength of the doctor and Severn to persuade him to lie down again, and a succession of coughing spells and hemorrhages reduced his strength to almost nothing. Physical pain and mental anguish were beyond any effort at discipline.

Joseph Severn nursed him night and day, attended to his every need, even cooked and cleaned and tended the fire, since the landlady in the back rooms refused to come near the contagion. As he sat by Keats's side and watched during his brief respites in sleep, Severn wrote the long letters to

England telling the Brawnes, Brown, Taylor and others of the imminence of John Keats's death.

Keats grew unbearably irritable, his flesh wasted away, and at times he was doubled up by waves of severe peristalsis. A dry cough became more and more frequent, and at night his sweating was severe. His body burned with fever.

In January he seemed to experience a slight rally, and Severn carried him in his arms to the next room, hoping that a change of scene would raise his spirits. But he sank quickly again. His suffering became so intense that he begged Severn for some laudanum they had purchased before leaving England.

"Let me have it," he pleaded. "Save me from the extended misery of a long illness."

Severn became so insecure and distressed about it that he turned the opium over to Dr. Clark for fear of yielding to Keats's entreaties.

By the beginning of February even Dr. Clark had to admit that John Keats had not long to live, and Joseph Severn remained at the poet's side almost without sleep. Toward the middle of the month, Keats grew calm and resigned, and for a brief moment his muse came back to him.

"Severn," he said, "will you put this on my grave: 'Here lies one whose name was writ in water.' Just that, and do not mention my name."

Around four in the afternoon on the twenty-third of February, 1821, Keats clung to Severn's hand and looked at him. Severn saw his eyes grow dim and heard the rattling in his chest as he strove to breathe.

"Lift me up," he gasped. "I shall die easy. Don't be frightened! Thank God it has come."

Joseph Severn cradled the poet in his arms as he sank slowly. By eleven o'clock that evening he was gone, slipped away into Endymion's eternal sleep.

CHAPTER XIV

Epilogue

JOHN KEATS lies buried in the Protestant Cemetery of Rome, in a far corner of its oldest portion. In accordance with his wishes his name does not appear on his tombstone, but its top is decorated by a lyre, and beneath it he is called a "Young English Poet—Whose name was writ in water." The curious Cestius Pyramid and a portion of the ancient Roman wall dominate the scene, and towering old cypress trees create an atmosphere of cathedral peace. Not far away, in a newer section, is the grave of Percy Bysshe Shelley who, at his own untimely death, was found to have a copy of the *Lamia* volume in his pocket, folded back to the page he had been reading.

When news of Keats's death reached Shelley, he wrote in Keats's memory his immortalizing *Adonais:*

Go thou to Rome,—at once the Paradise,
The grave, the city, and the wilderness;

And where its wrecks like shattered mountains rise,
And flowering weeds, and fragrant copses dress
The bones of Desolation's nakedness
Pass, till the spirit of the spot shall lead
Thy footsteps to a slope of green access
Where, like an infant's smile, over the dead
A light of laughing flowers along the grass is spread . . .

Glossary of Poetry Terms
Used in This Volume

ALEXANDRINE. A line of six iambic, or four anapestic, measures (see meter), usually combined for effect with shorter lines.

ALLEGORY. A figure of speech in which one image is substituted for another: animals talking and behaving like persons; human beings representing concepts like virtue and courage.

BALLAD. A narrative poem written in a song lyric pattern.

CANTO. Principal part of a long poem.

COUPLET. A pair of verses or lines occurring together and matched in meter and rhyme.

ELEGIAC. Lyrical verse patterned after the ancient Greek and Roman dirges.

EPITHALAMIUM. A wedding song.

IMAGERY. The creation of clear pictures in the mind of the reader.

MEASURE (*or* FOOT). Structural unit of a line of poetry. A line of poetry usually has a prescribed number of measures or feet.

234

For example:

monometer is a line of poetry containing only one measure
dimeter, two measures
trimeter, three measures
tetrameter, four measures
pentameter, five measures
hexameter, six measures

METER. The pattern of a measure. The principal patterns are: *anapestic*, in which each measure contains two unaccented syllables followed by an accented one, often called the galloping rhythm:

The Assyrian came down like the wolf on the fold (Byron)
dactylic, in which each measure contains an accented syllable followed by two unaccented syllables:

This is the forest primeval. The murmuring (Longfellow)
iambic, in which every second, fourth, sixth, etc., syllable is accented:

Small, busy flames (Keats)
trochaic, in which every first, third, fifth, etc., syllable is accented:

In thy western halls of gold (Keats)

ODE. A lyrical poem, very like a hymn, used by the ancient Greeks to be sung by choral groups.

RHYME SCHEME. A plan of combining different words with identical sound endings, usually at the ends of lines. The rhyme scheme of a poem is identified by calling all the endings of one sound *a*, the second *b*, etc.:

> Chief of organic numbers! *a*
> Old Scholar of the Spheres *b*
> Thy spirit never slumbers, *a*
> But rolls about our ears *b*
> (Keats)

ROUNDELAY. A lyrical poem or song in which a simple stanza pattern is repeated again and again.

SONNET. A poem of fourteen lines of iambic pentameter for which there are several rhyme schemes. The Italian, or Petrarchan, sonnet is rhymed: *abbaabba cdecde* with some slight variation in the last six lines. The Spenserian sonnet is rhymed: *ababbcbccdcdee.* The Shakespearean sonnet is rhymed: *ababcdcdefefgg.*

STANZA. A set of poetic lines grouped to form a pattern.

VERSE. A single line of poetry.

Selected Bibliography

The following selected bibliography is recommended to the reader who wishes to continue his interest in the subject of John Keats:

Adami, Maria. *Fanny Keats*. New Haven, 1938.
Altick, Richard D. *The Cowden Clarkes*. London, 1948.
Blunden, Edmund. *Leigh Hunt and His Circle*. New York, 1930.
———. *Leigh Hunt's "Examiner" Examined*. London, 1928.
Brawne, Fanny. *Letters of Fanny Brawne to Fanny Keats 1820-1824*, Edited by Fred Edgcumbe. New York, 1937.
Brown, Charles Armitage. *Life of John Keats*. London, 1937.
Bushnell, Nelson S. *A Walk After John Keats*. New York, 1936.
Chew, Samuel C. *A Literary History of England, Volume IV, The Nineteenth Century and After*. New York, 1948.
Clarke, Charles and Mary Cowden. *Recollections of Writers*. London, 1878.
Clarke, Mary Cowden. *The Life and Labours of Vincent Novello by His Daughter*. London, 1863.

237

Deutsch, Babette. *Poetry Handbook, A Dictionary of Terms.* New York, 1957.

Frankel, Hermann. *Ovid: A Poet Between Two Worlds.* Los Angeles, 1945.

Gittings, Robert. *John Keats, The Living Year.* Cambridge, 1954.

——. *The Mask of Keats, A Study of Problems.* Cambridge, 1956.

Hale-White, Sir William. *Keats as Doctor and Patient.* London, 1938.

Hewlett, Dorothy. *A Life of John Keats.* New York, 1950.

Howe, P. P. *The Life of William Hazlitt.* London, 1922.

Hunt, Leigh. *The Autobiography of Leigh Hunt.* Edited by J. E. Morpurgo. New York, 1948.

Jones, H. S. V. *A Spenser Handbook.* New York, 1930.

Keats, John. *Anatomical and Physiological Note Book.* Edited by Maurice Buxton Forman. London, 1934.

——. *The Letters of John Keats.* Edited by Maurice Buxton Forman. London, 1931.

——. *The Letters of John Keats 1814-1821.* Edited by Hyder Edward Rollins. Cambridge, 1958.

——. *Life, Letters and Literary Remains of John Keats.* Edited by Richard Milnes. New York, 1848.

——. *The Poetical Works of John Keats.* Edited by H. W. Garrod. Oxford, 1958.

——. *The Selected Letters of John Keats.* Edited by Lionel Trilling. Garden City, 1951.

Lowell, Amy. *John Keats.* Boston, 1925.

Lucas, E. V. *The Life of Charles Lamb.* New York, 1905.

Miller, Barnette. *Leigh Hunt's Relations with Byron, Shelley and Keats.* New York, 1910.

Muir, Kenneth. *John Keats, A Reassessment.* Liverpool, 1958.

Murchie, Guy. *The Spirit of Place in Keats.* London, 1955.

Murry, John Middleton. *Keats.* New York, 1955.

Olney, Clarke. *Benjamin Robert Haydon, Historical Painter.* Athens, 1952.

Parson, Donald. *Portraits of Keats.* New York, 1954.

Peck, Walter Edwin. *Shelley, His Life and Work.* Boston, 1927.

Rannie, David Watson. *Wordsworth and His Circle.* London, 1907.

Raymond, Ernest. *Two Gentlemen of Rome, The Story of Keats and Shelley.* London, 1952.

Richardson, Joanna. *Fanny Brawne.* New York, 1952.

Rogers, Neville (compiler). *Keats, Shelley & Rome.* London, 1957.

Rollins, Hyder Edward. *The Keats Circle, Letters and Papers 1816-1878.* Cambridge, 1948.

Rossetti, William Michael. *Life of John Keats.* London, 1887.

Sharp, William. *Life and Letters of Joseph Severn.* New York, 1892.

Thorpe, Clarence D. *et al* (editors). *The Major English Romantic Poets.* Carbondale, 1957.

Wasserman, Earl R. *The Finer Tone, Keats' Major Poems.* Baltimore, 1953.

Weller, Earle Vonard. *Keats and Mary Tighe.* New York, 1928.

Index

241